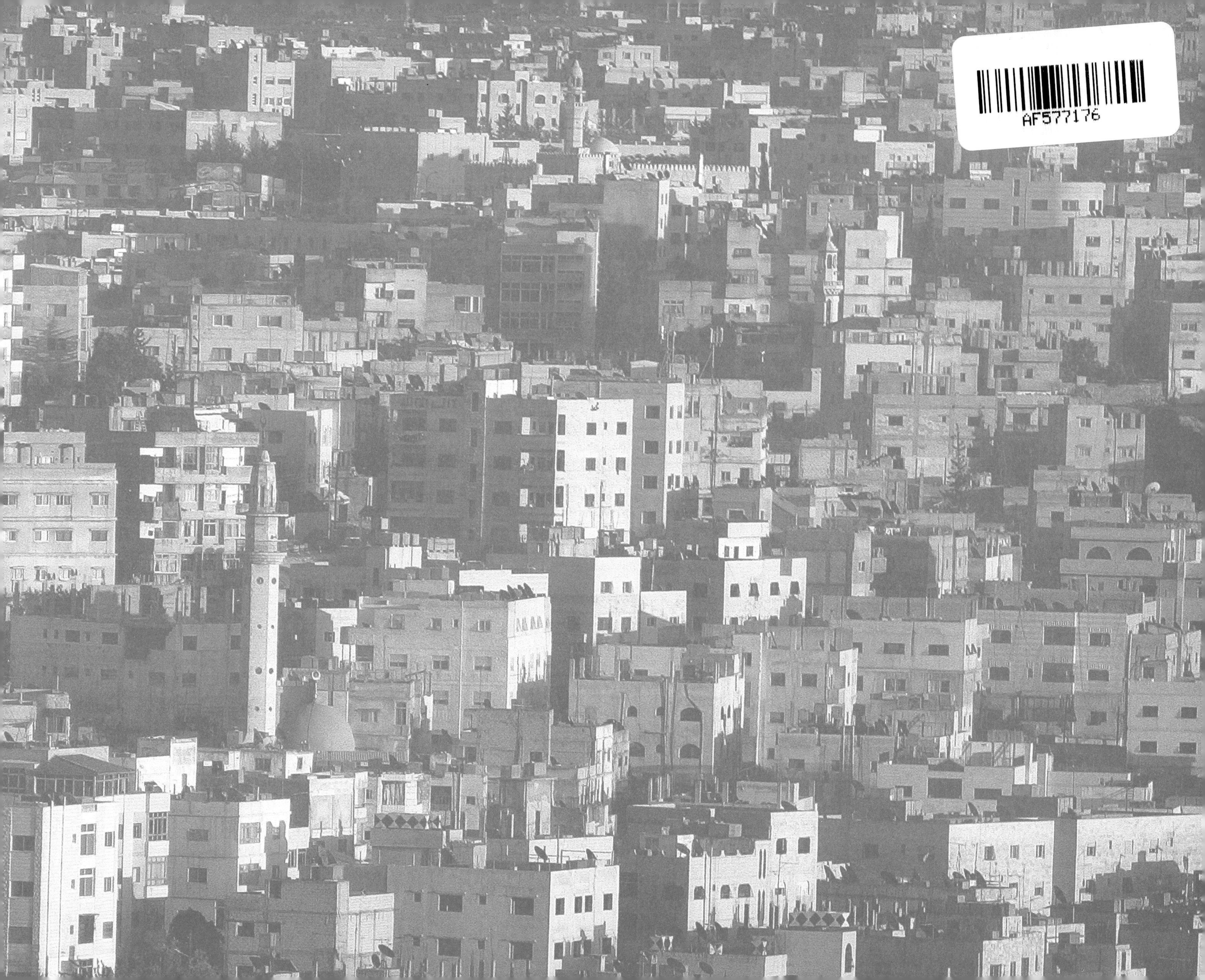

land of contrasts jordan

photography and text
by George Fischer

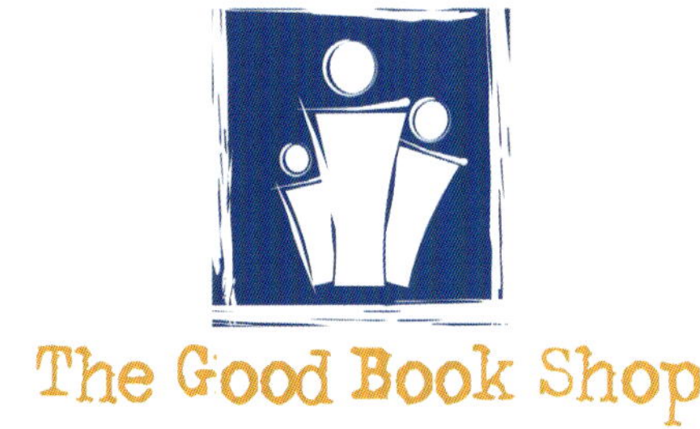

The Good Book Shop

Nimbus Publishing Limited
PO Box 9166
Halifax, NS B3K 5MB
902-455-4286

Jordan and Middle East Distributor:
The Good Book Shop
First Circle, Amman Jordan
+962-6-4613939
info@bookshop.jo

Printed in China

Design: Catharine Barker, National Graphics, Toronto, ON

Library and Archives Canada Cataloguing in Publication

Fischer, George, 1954-
Jordan : a land of contrasts / photography by George Fischer.

ISBN 978-1-55109-720-6

1. Jordan--Pictorial works. I. Title.

DS153.F48 2009 956.9504'40222 C2008-907517-X

ACKNOWLEDGMENTS: Photographing in Jordan has been a wonderful experience, and producing this book was a joy! I would like to thank the lovely and beautiful Desert Queens – Elina Taji, Luma Khatib, and Jennifer McDonald – for modeling with such patience and perseverance at the desert castles in Eastern Jordan. Thank you also to Lubna Zawaideh, her son, and Saed Zawaideh for modeling. To Tala Bani Hani and Banan Jebril, thank you both for your friendly smiles at Royal Jordanian Airlines. For the great hike in the Dana Reserve and in Aqaba, a big thanks to Mona Al Jamal. To Muna Haddad, Ahmed Hmoud, who invited me into their homes to experience the genuine Jordanian hospitality – shukran! Maram Mazahreh, Tohama Nabulsi and Rasha Hamshawi – you were amazing in the co-ordination and planning of all the photo shoots and for fooling me into believing that a night out for dinner or for my favorite snack of kunafa or fruit juice was not a photo shoot in some way! This book would not have been possible had it not been for Frank and Mary Lafleche inviting me to experience Jordan first hand, and Malia Asfour and Gisele Abrahao of the JTB North America for their confidence in me. For the detail of editing, my thanks to Rula Hijazeen Karam. To Hatem Zaal, who drove me to the four corners of Jordan, and who was never afraid to get his jeep stuck in the desert no matter how lost we were – a heartfelt thank you. Thanks go as well to Nayef H. Al Fayez director of the JTB in Jordan, Yola Isaac and Ingo Roessler of Royal Jordanian Airlines, and Bruno Huber of Mövenpick Hotels & Resorts for their photo, inset page 57. Always last but never forgotten, thanks to my long time photographic assistant, Jean Lepage, for his patience.

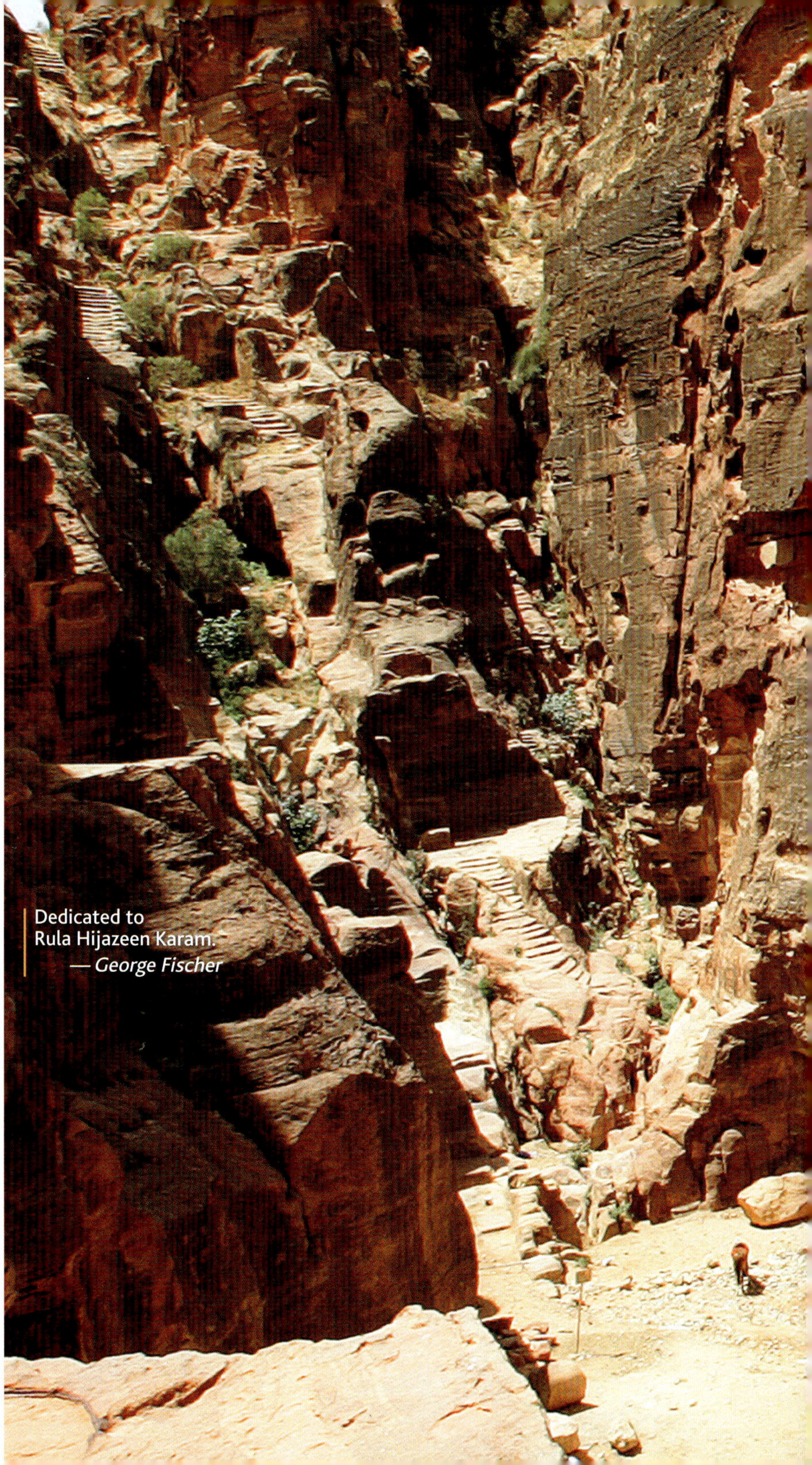

Dedicated to
Rula Hijazeen Karam.
— George Fischer

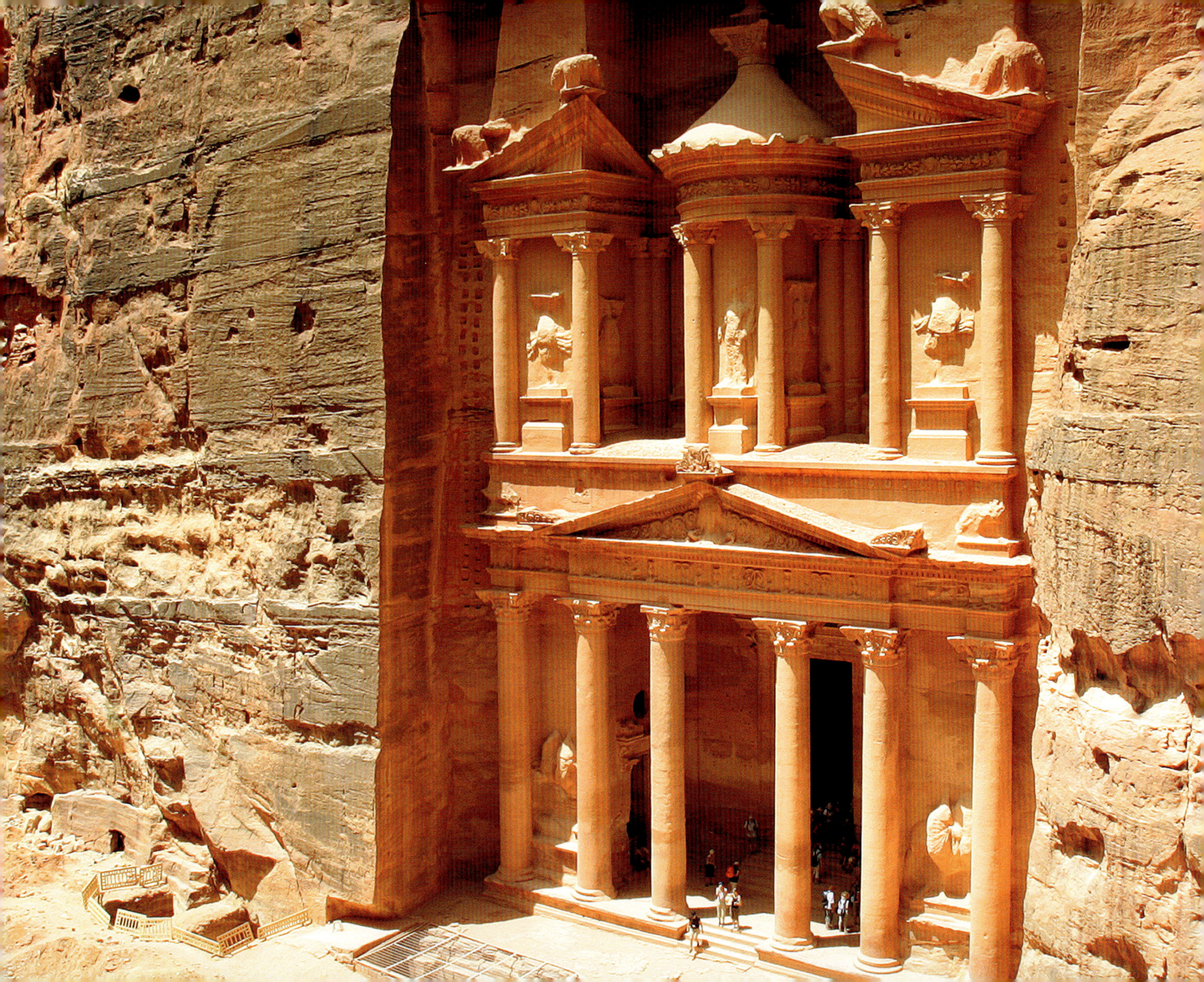

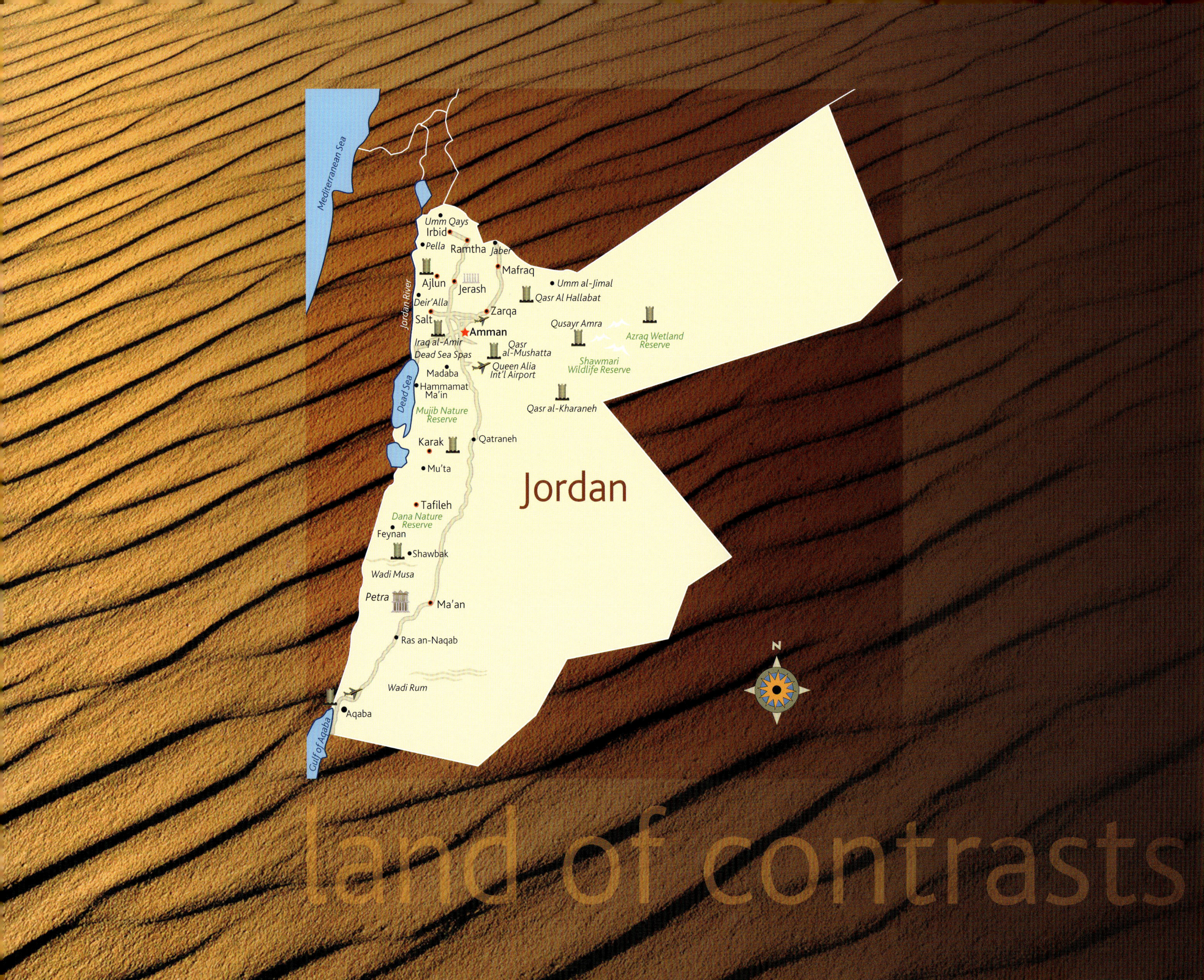

Mediterranean Sea
Umm Qays
Irbid
Pella
Ramtha
Jaber
Mafraq
Ajlun
Jerash
Umm al-Jimal
Qasr Al Hallabat
Jordan River
Deir'Alla
Zarqa
Salt
Amman
Qusayr Amra
Azraq Wetland Reserve
Iraq al-Amir
Dead Sea Spas
Qasr al-Mushatta
Madaba
Queen Alia Int'l Airport
Shawmari Wildlife Reserve
Dead Sea
Hammamat Ma'in
Mujib Nature Reserve
Qasr al-Kharaneh
Karak
Qatraneh
Mu'ta
Jordan
Tafileh
Dana Nature Reserve
Feynan
Shawbak
Wadi Musa
Petra
Ma'an
Ras an-Naqab
Wadi Rum
Aqaba
Gulf of Aqaba
N
land of contrasts

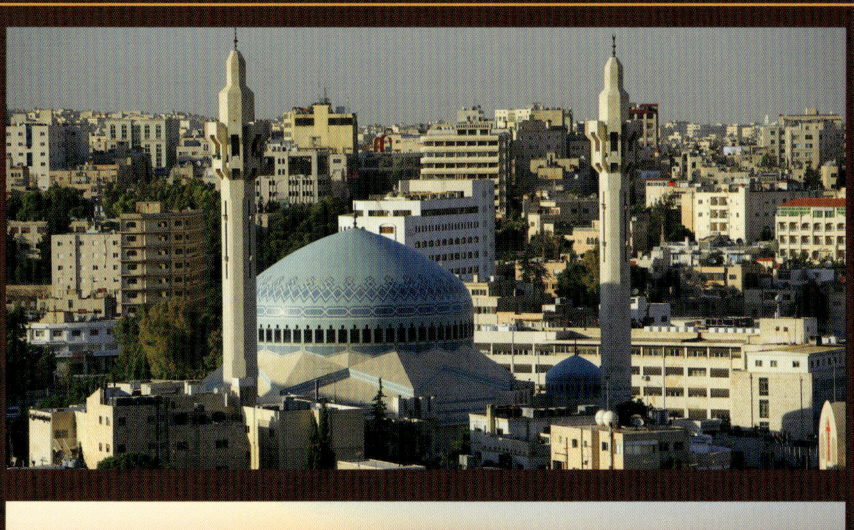

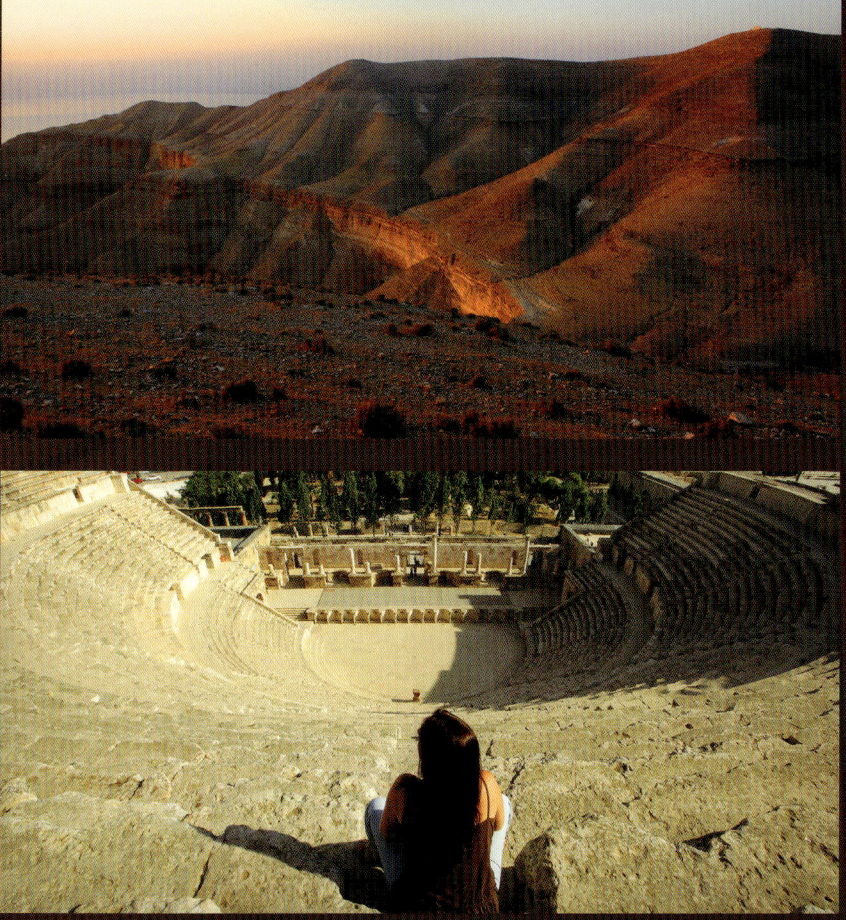

I am proud to present this lovely book about Jordan—my labor of love for this land of contrasts, wonder and enchantment.

Through the prism of my passion for this country, I have recorded matchless images and timeless stories that I am delighted to share with you.

The Hashemite Kingdom of Jordan is a well-traveled bridge between east and west, desert and sea, ancient and modern. From the verdant Jordan Valley to the arid canyons of Wadi Rum and the indigo depths of the Red Sea of Aqaba, I see through my lens an extraordinary world. Here, visitors can follow in the footsteps of prophets and disciples, float in the Dead Sea's healing waters and explore historical Petra, the Jewel of Jordan.

Not to be underestimated are the country's moderate weather, world-class facilities and gracious hospitality. These features are vital to making Jordan the ideal destination for those seeking the experience of a lifetime.

I trust that browsing through this pictorial collection will be your first step in exploring this splendid country.

— *George Fischer*

Have a good journey.

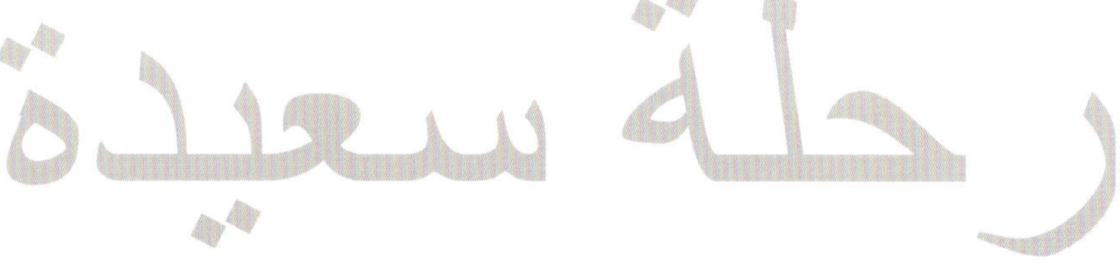

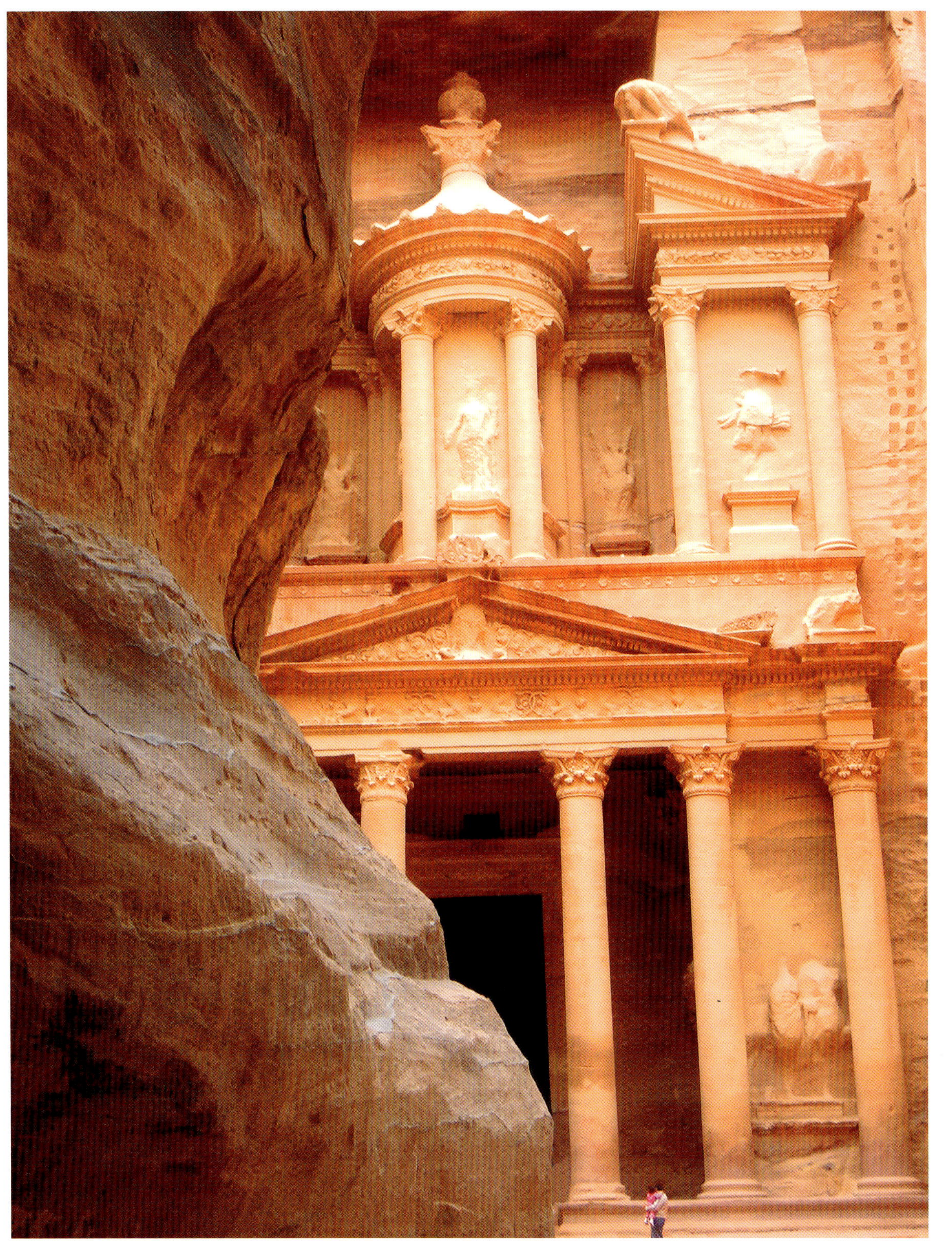

An enchanting landscape of red sands and monumental sandstone peaks are "vast, echoing and godlike", as Lawrence of Arabia described the silent, immense desert panoramas of the Wadi Rum.

Through *Al-Siq*, the colonnaded entry to Jordan's most famous rose-red city of Petra, we see the Treasury's magnificent tomb-like facade towering over visitors.

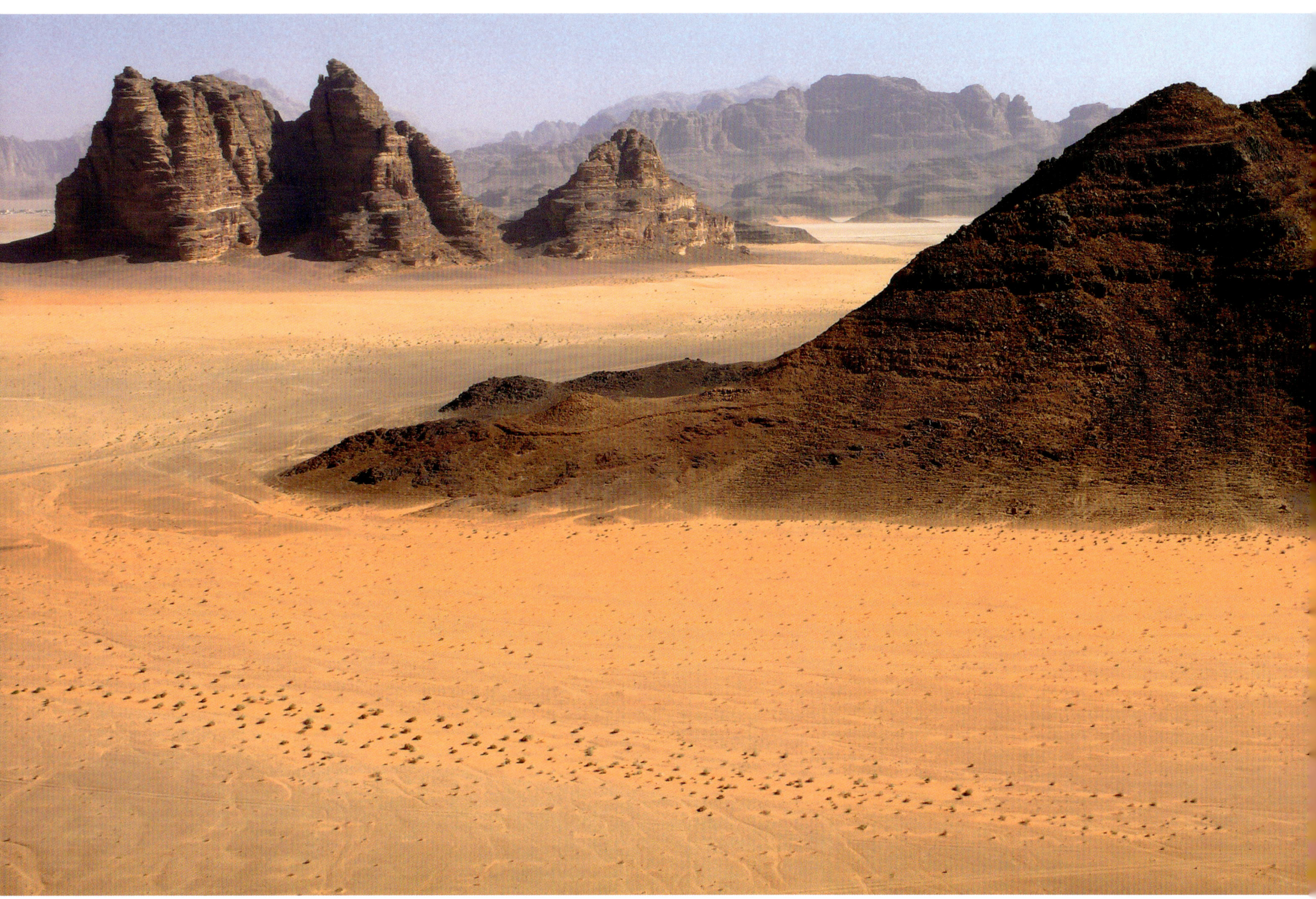

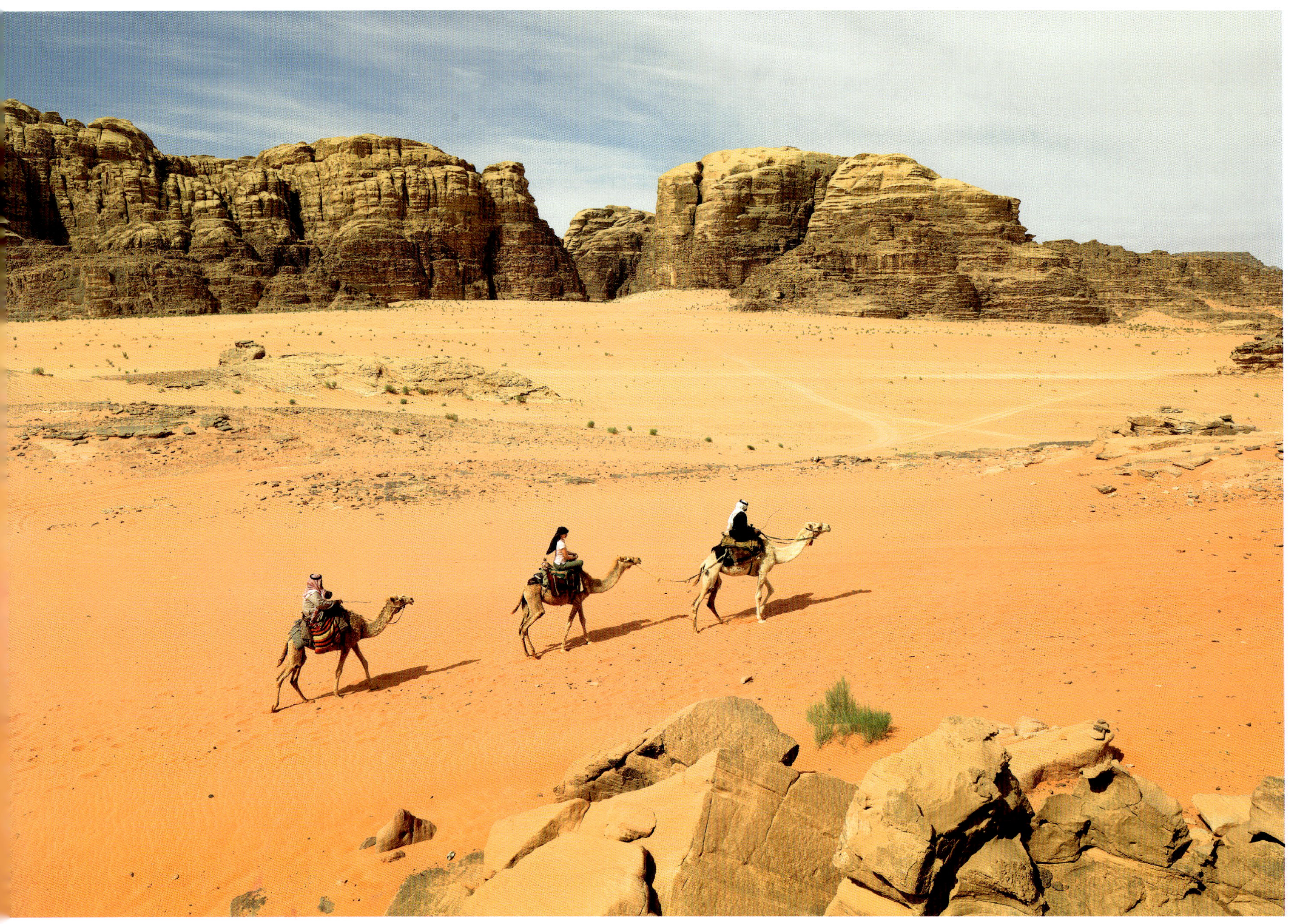

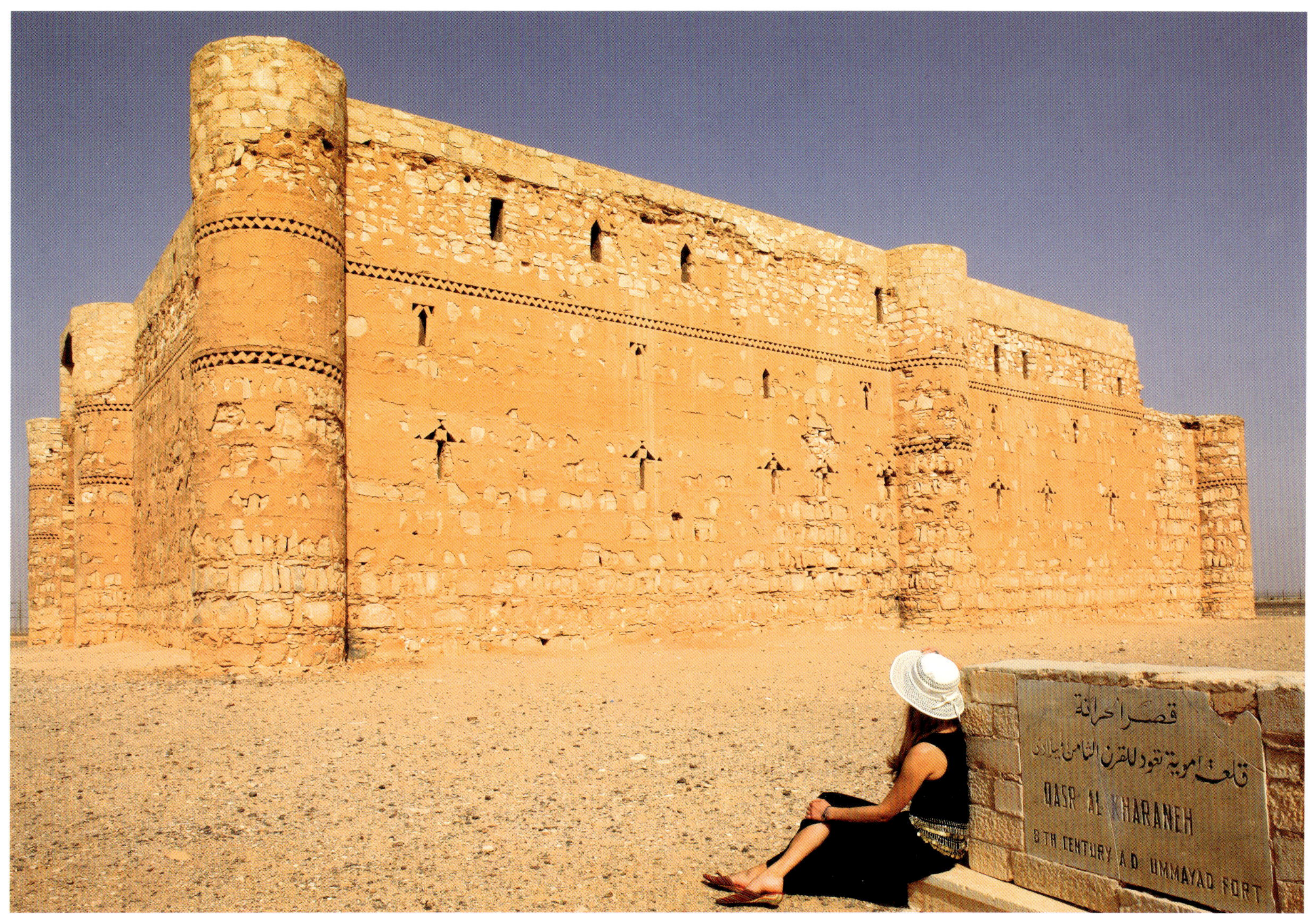

Camel safaris are a popular activity for adventure seeking tourists in the Wadi Rum. Who can resist the gentle swaying and shuffling of these "ships of the desert" as they glide through the steep dunes?

Isolated in the Badia Desert, the 2-storey palace of Qasr al-Kharaneh is a testament to the fine Islamic art and architecture of the 8th century. Extremely well preserved, its looming presence on the barren landscape is not to be forgotten.

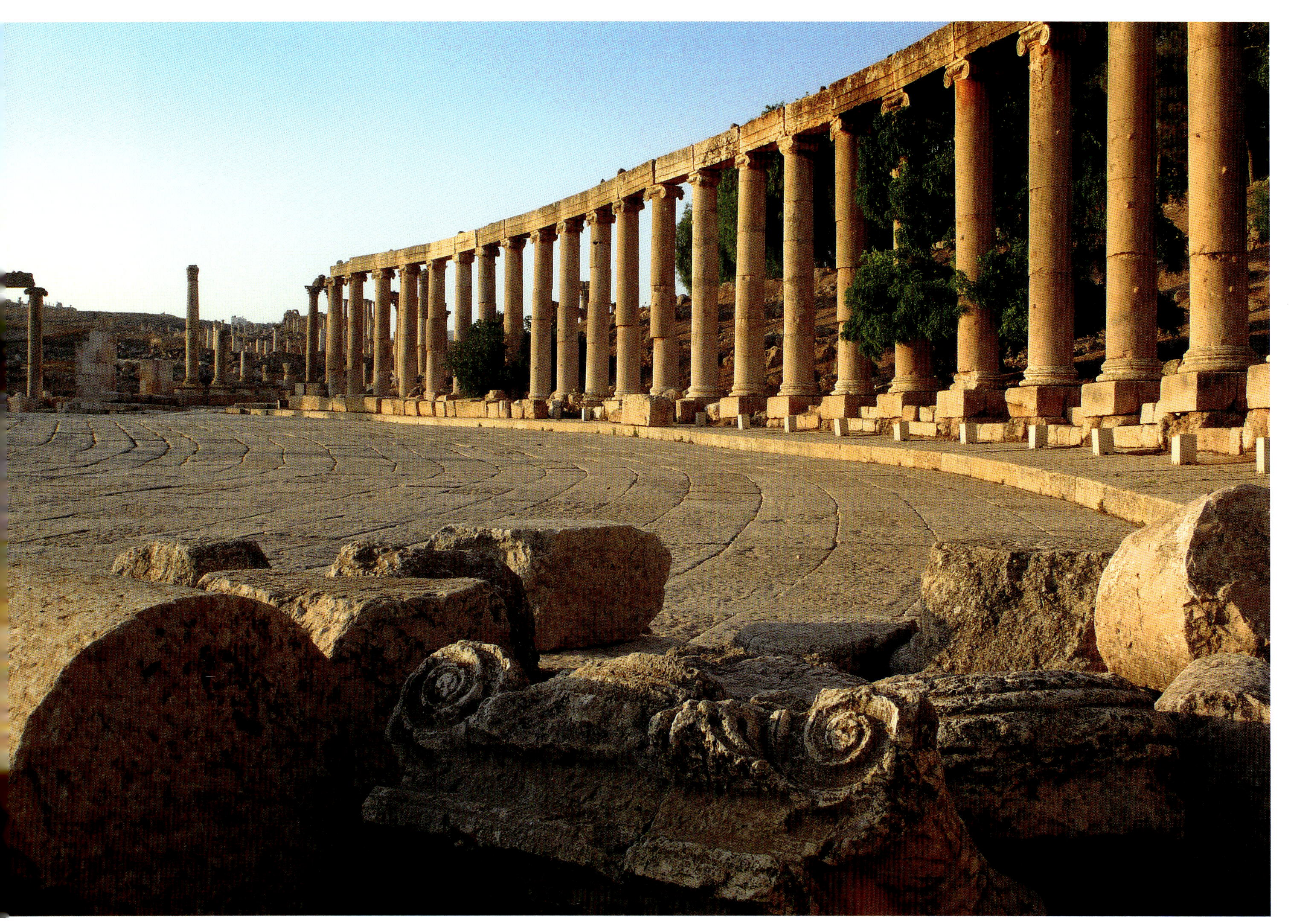

An outpost of the Roman Empire in the Middle East, the city of Jerash is a well preserved pearl of beauty situated in the northern hills of Jordan. Containing a treasure of colonnaded streets and pillars reaching up to the land of gods, it was considered the Rome away from Rome.

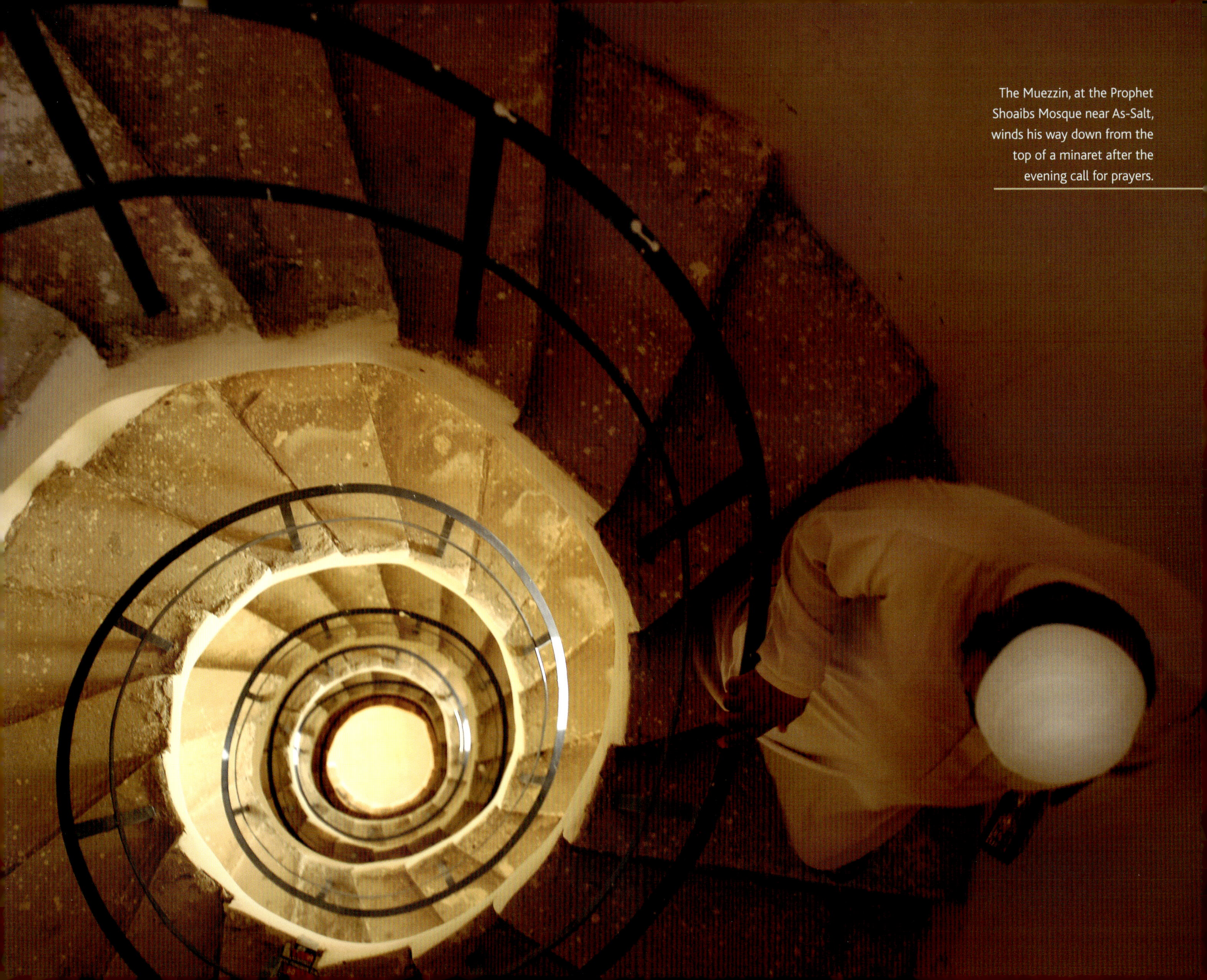

The Muezzin, at the Prophet Shoaibs Mosque near As-Salt, winds his way down from the top of a minaret after the evening call for prayers.

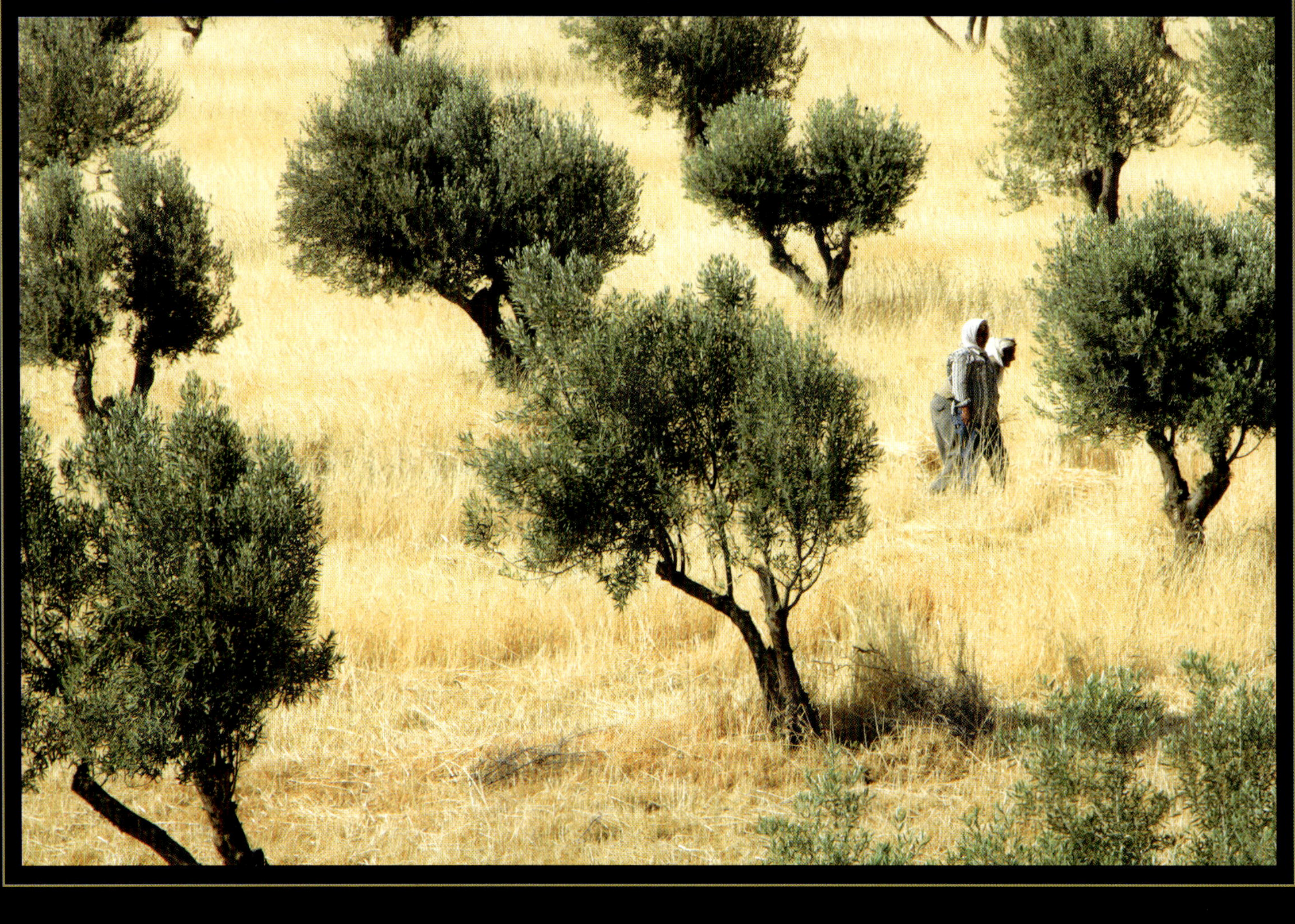

A family near Madaba traverses a golden field dotted with olive trees.
During the September harvest, fruit is picked and turned into olive oil

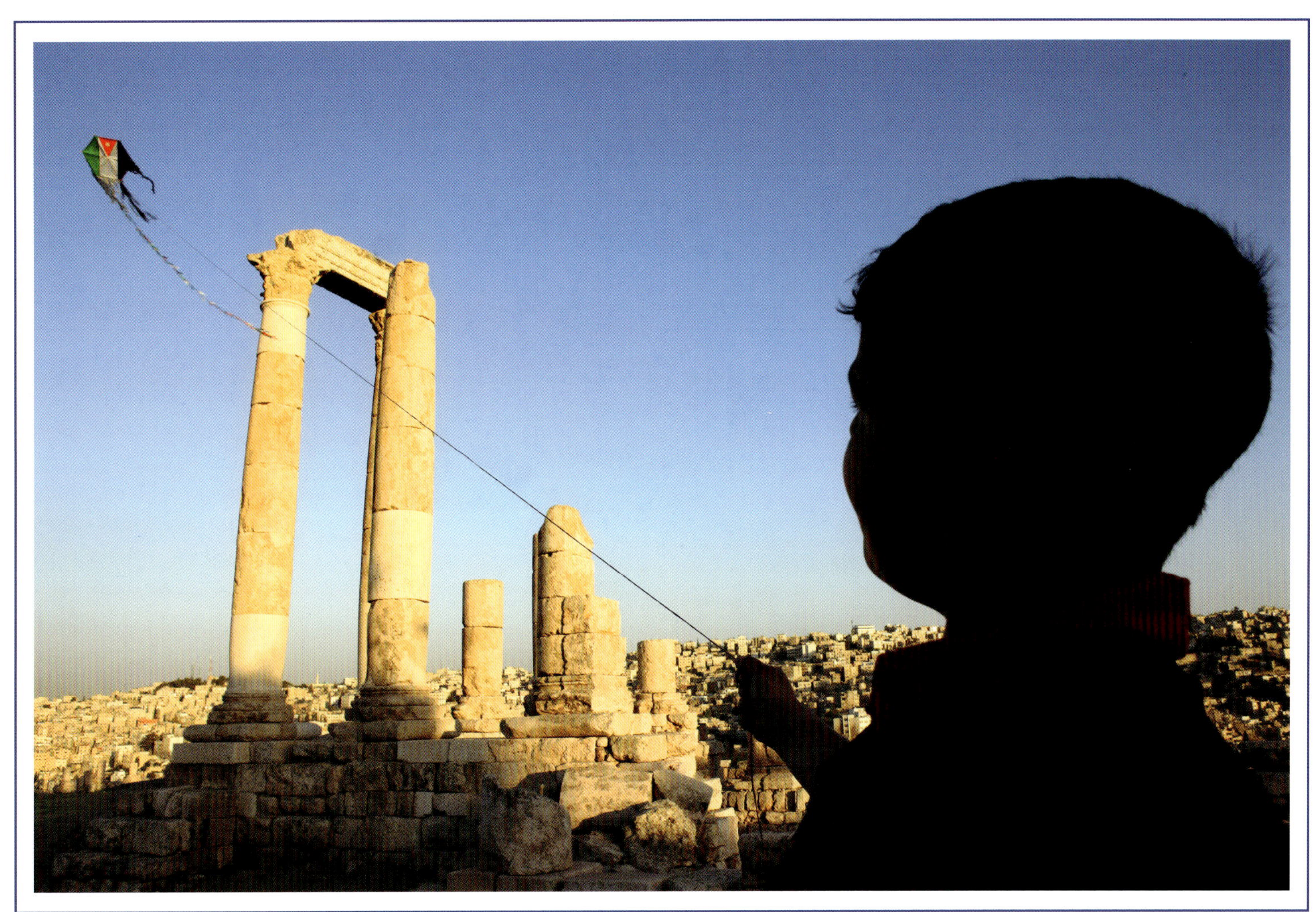

A gust of wind and a skillful tug of the wrist send this colorful kite soaring among the ancient columns of the Temple of Hercules on Citadel Hill – Jabal al-Qal'ah in Amman – the capital of Jordan.

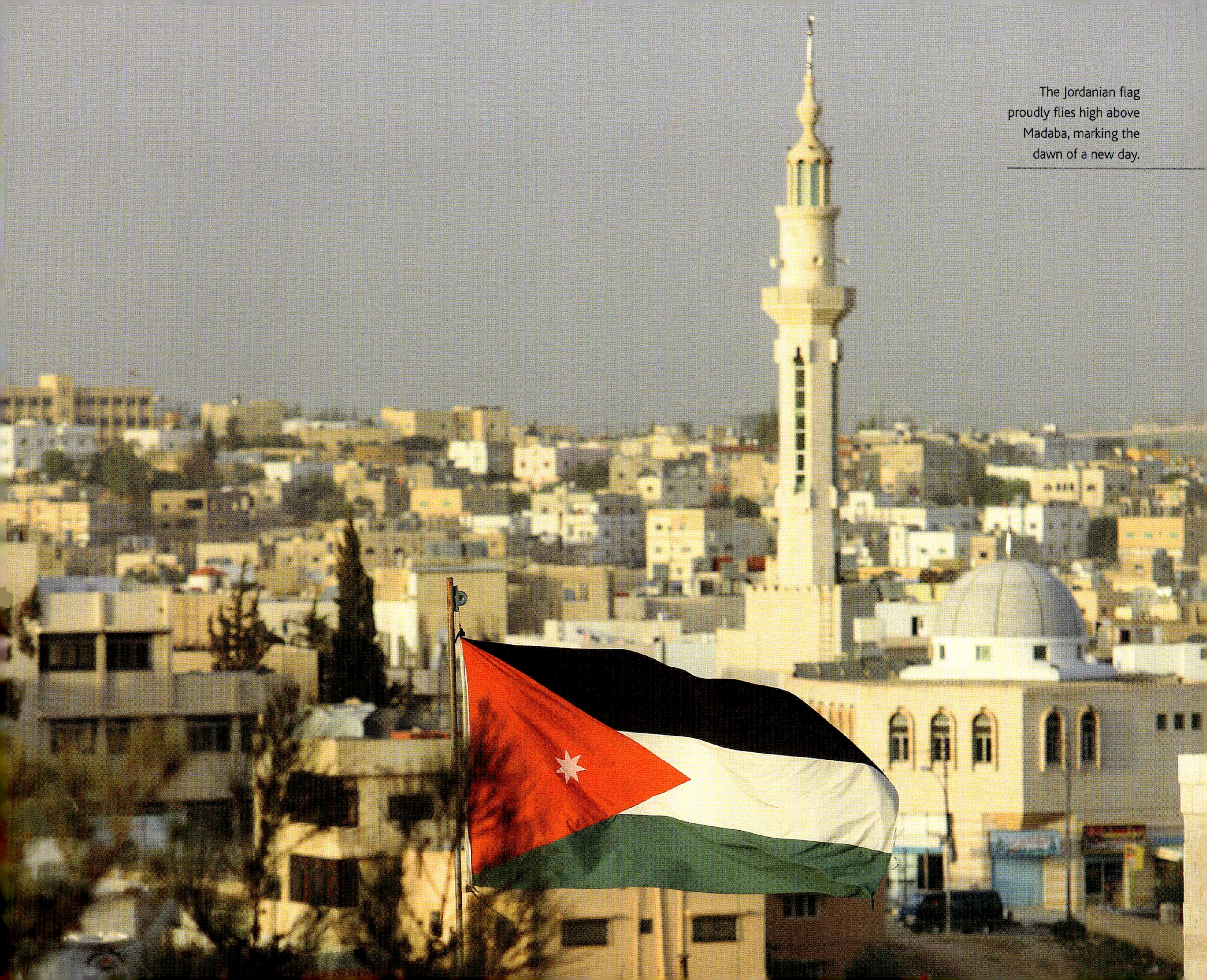

The Jordanian flag proudly flies high above Madaba, marking the dawn of a new day.

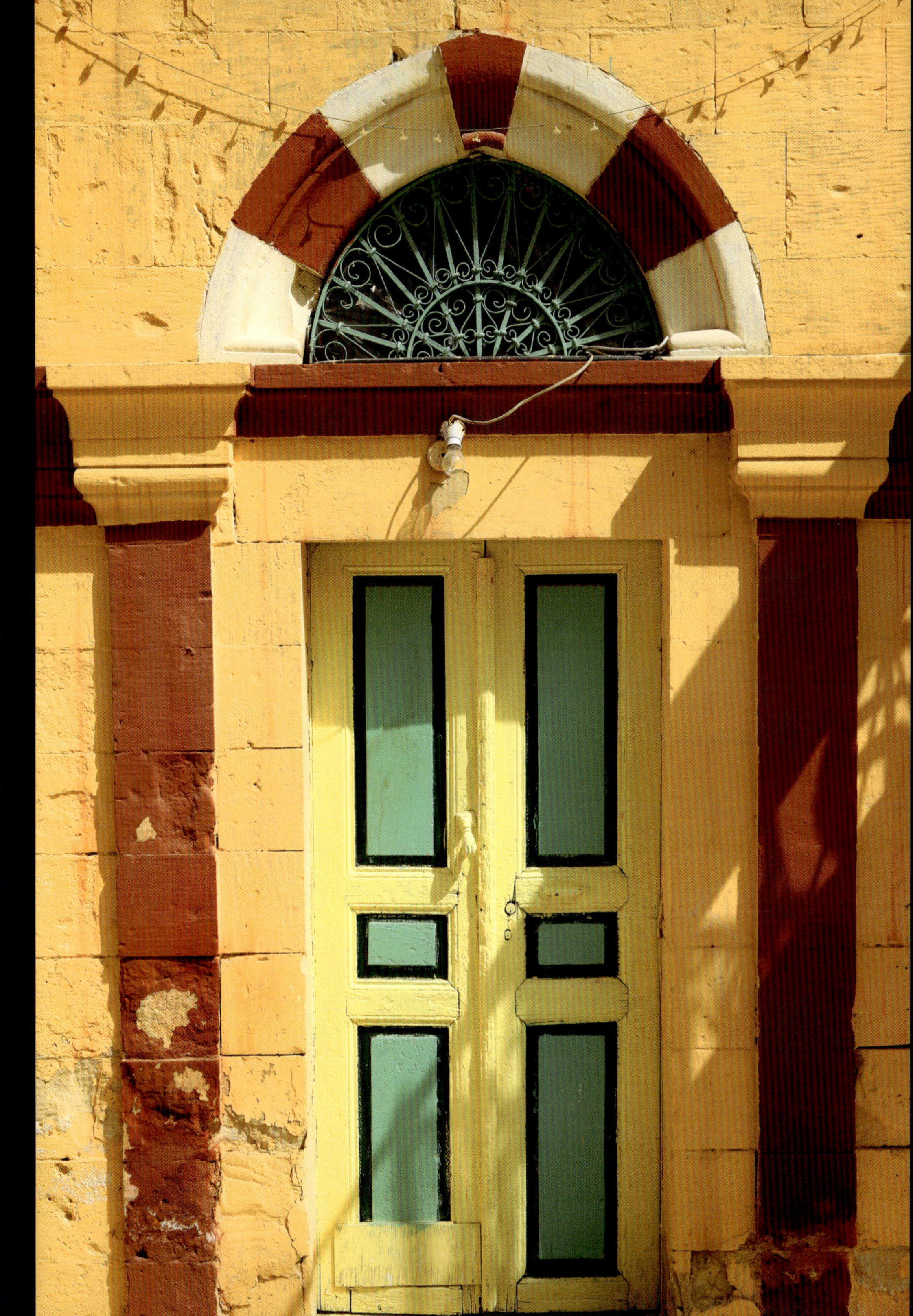

Renowned for its Ottoman architecture, this arched entry is a fine example of the brightly colored doors, windows and facades that adorn the steep, narrow backstreets of As-Salt – the former capital of Jordan.

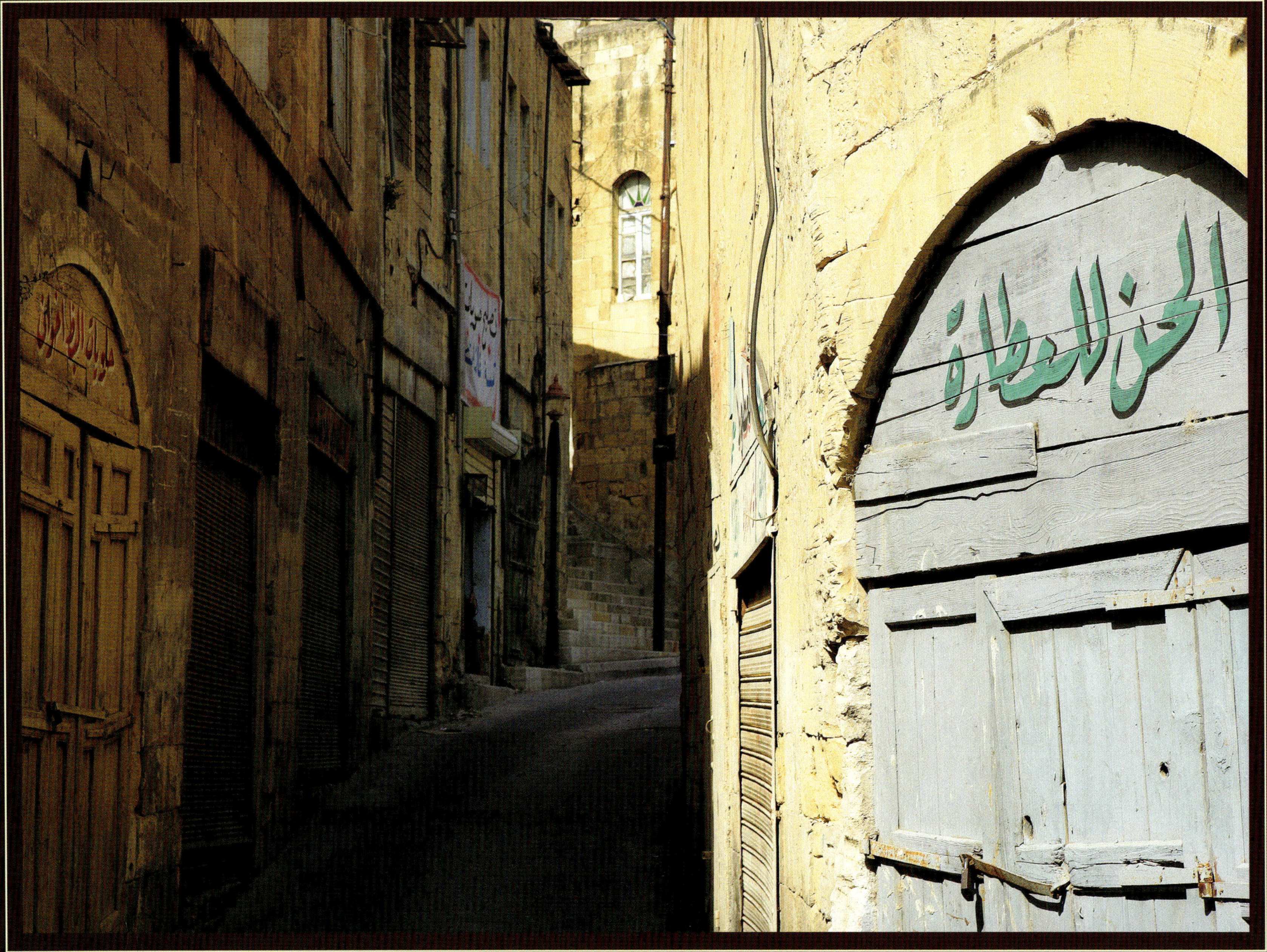

During Friday prayers in As-Salt, the winding lanes empty and shop doors are tightly closed while worshippers attend the ornate mosque on Hammam Street.

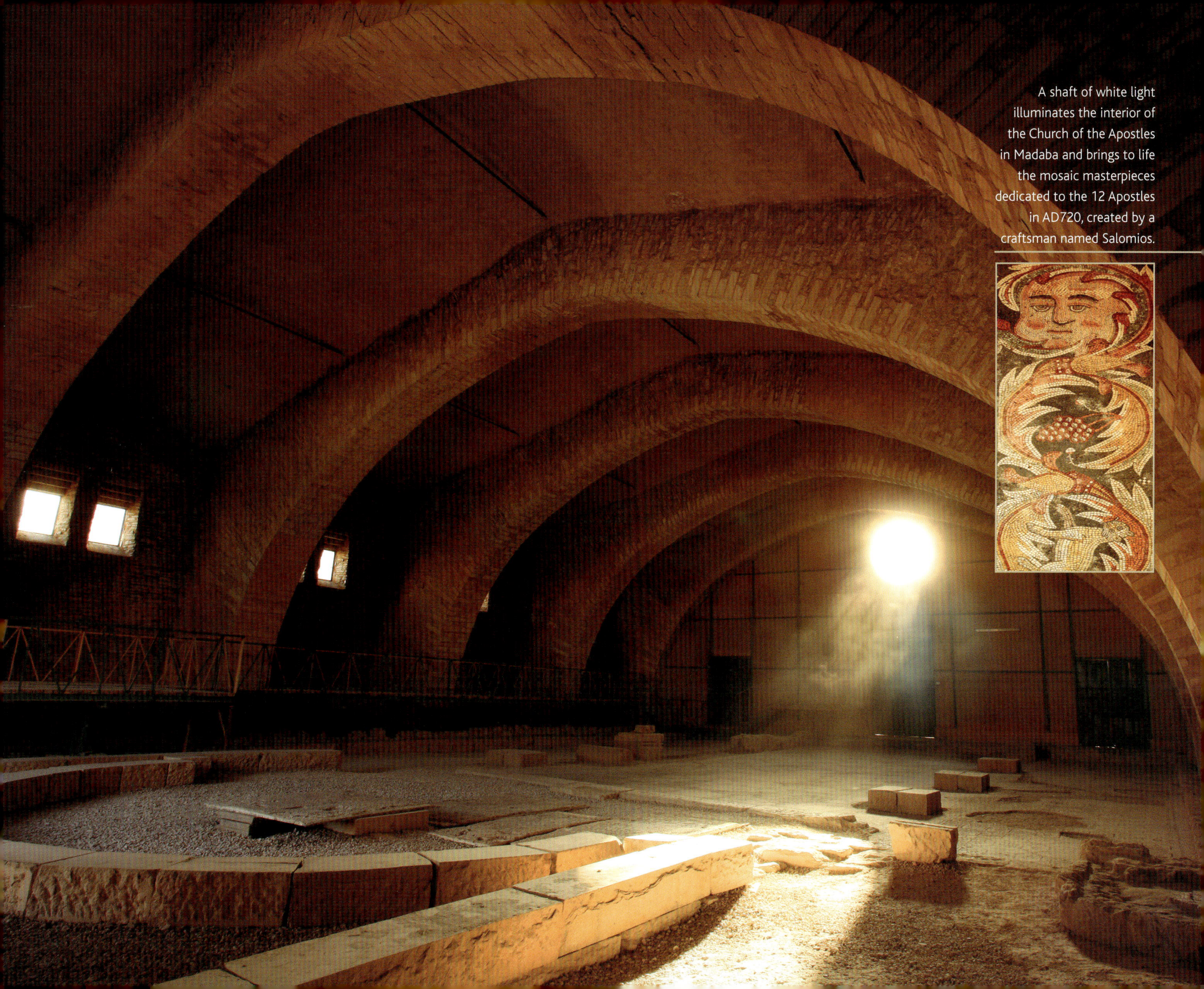

A shaft of white light illuminates the interior of the Church of the Apostles in Madaba and brings to life the mosaic masterpieces dedicated to the 12 Apostles in AD720, created by a craftsman named Salomios.

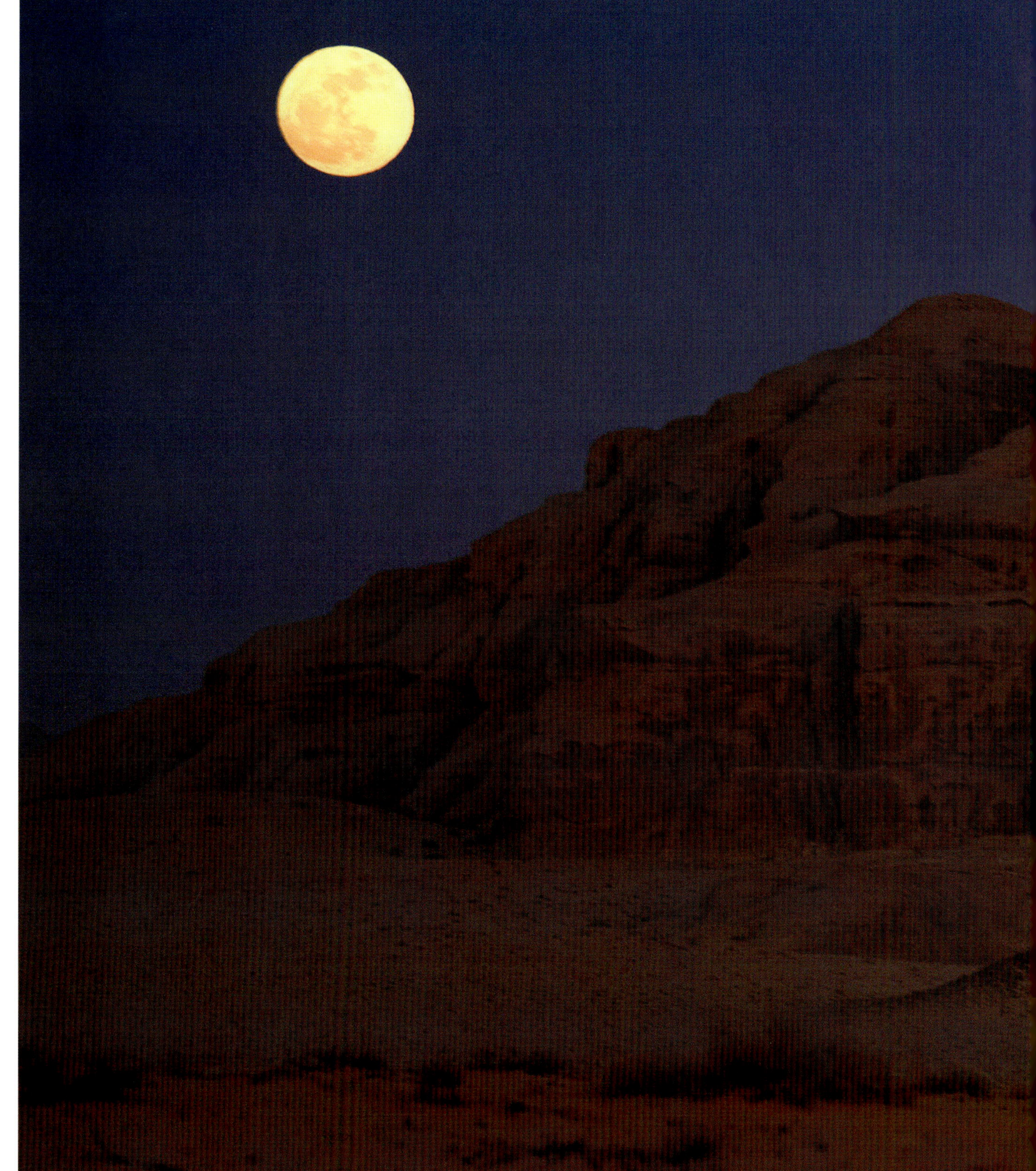

The lunar-like landscape of the Wadi Rum becomes even more magical as a full moon rises over the craggy basalt and sandstone sentinels that rise to heights of over 800 m from the desert floor.

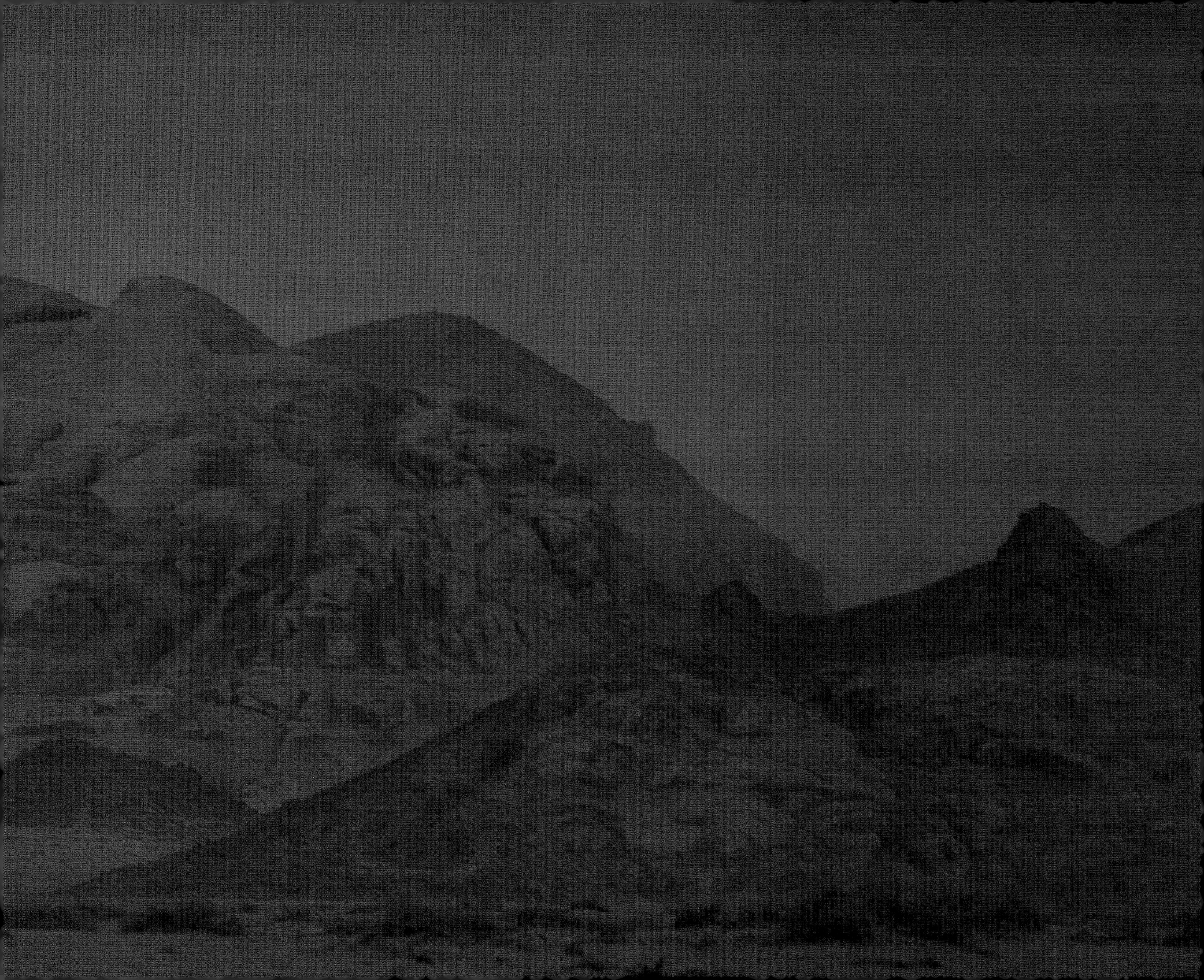

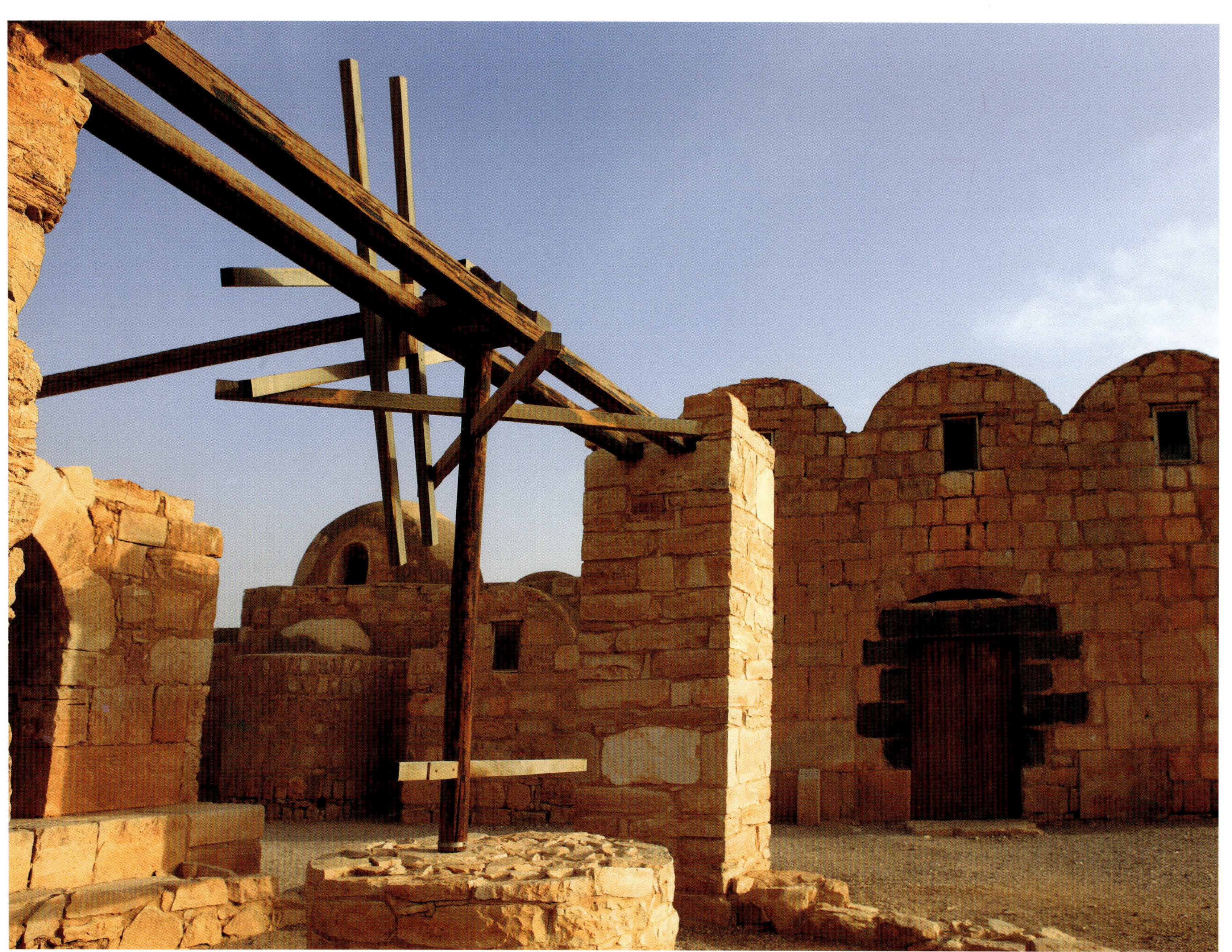

Lost in the desert expanse of eastern Jordan lies the Qusayr Amra, one of the desert castles of Jordan – a jewel containing treasured frescoes that adorn the vaulted ceilings. It was built as a hunting lodge for Caliph Walid I and is a World UNESCO Heritage site.

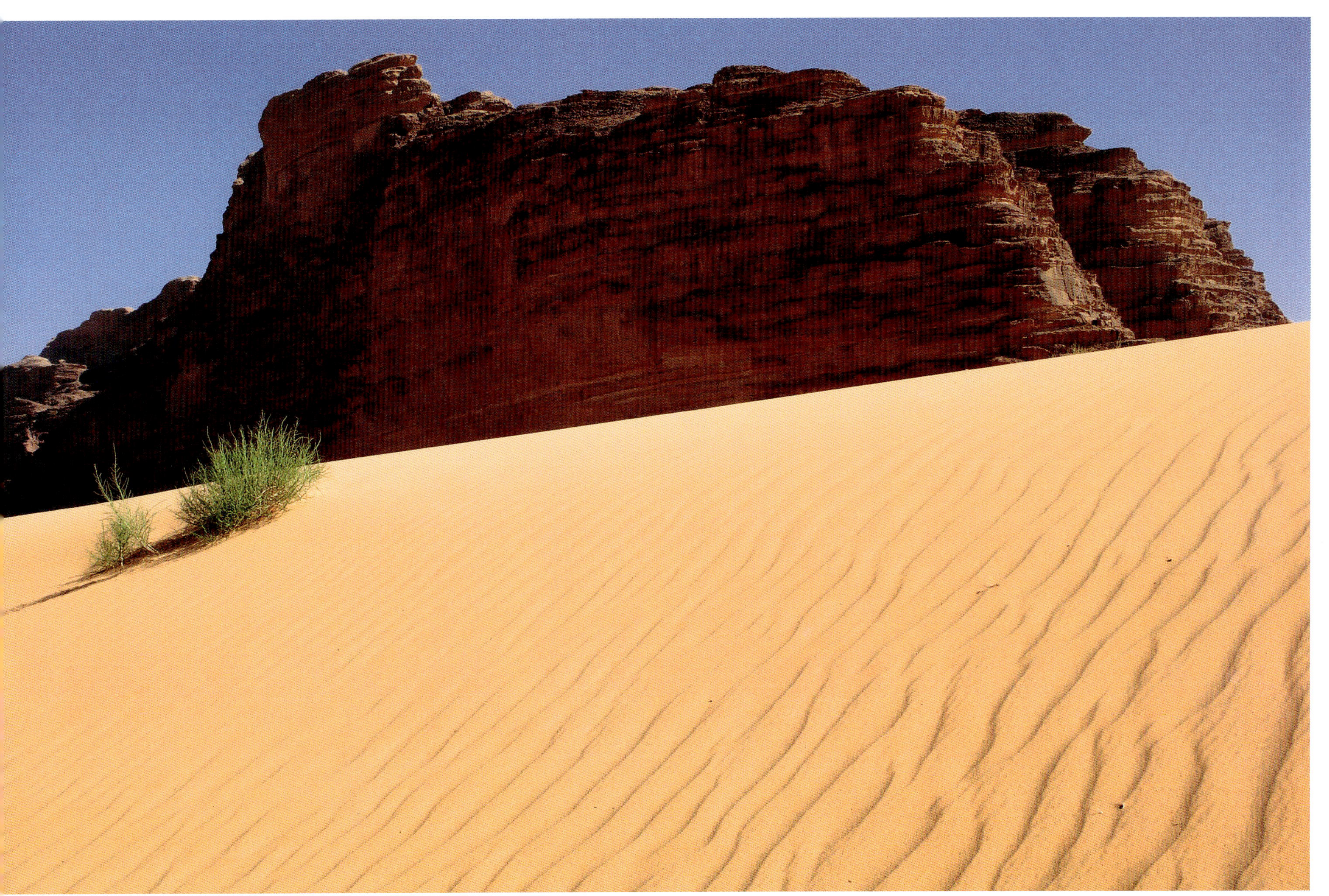

The untouched, shifting sand dunes of the Wadi Rum appear to be an inhospitable terrain, but beneath the sand, fairly close to the surface, there are numerous springs and aquifers bringing to life various shrubs and grasses.

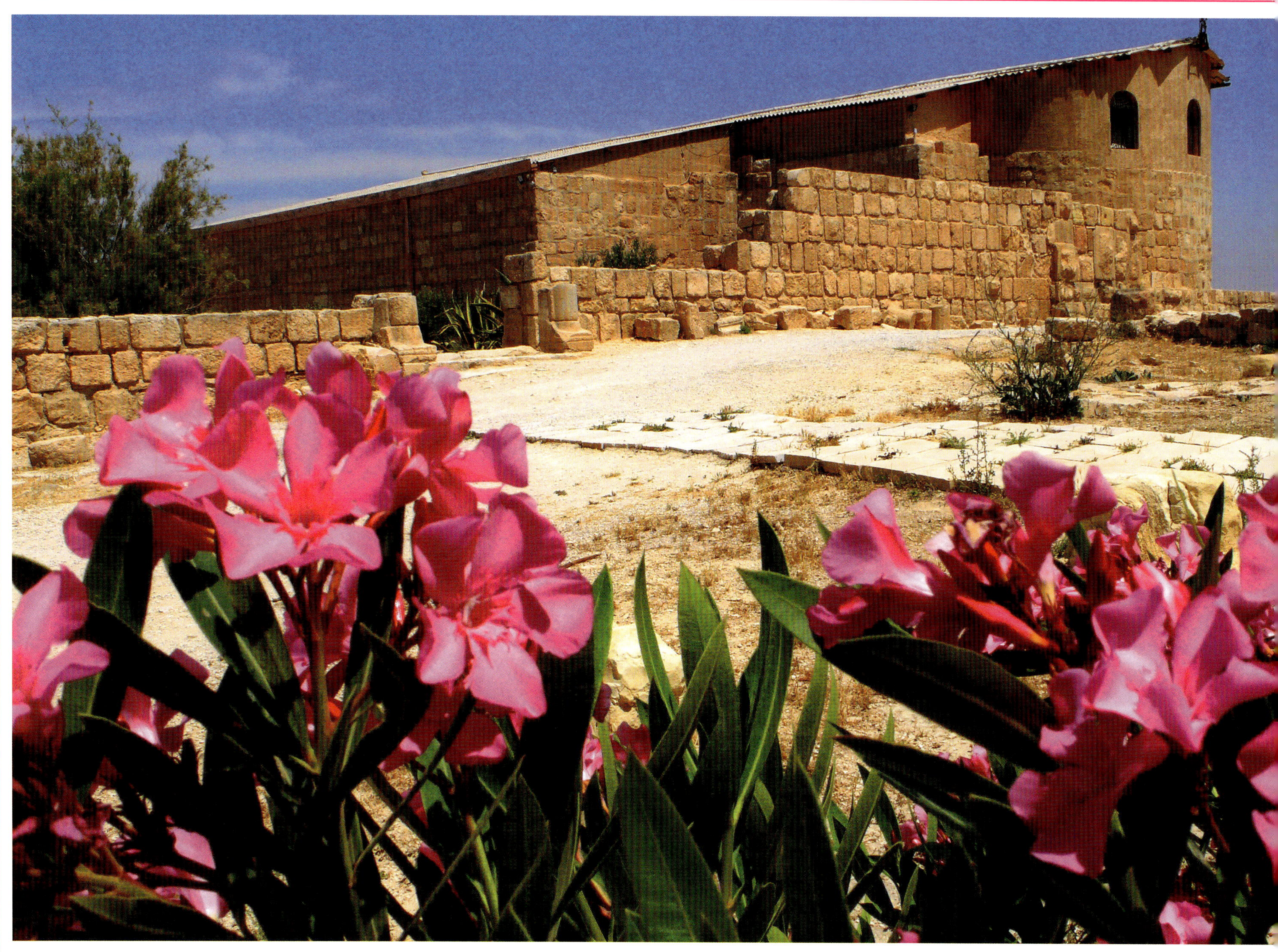

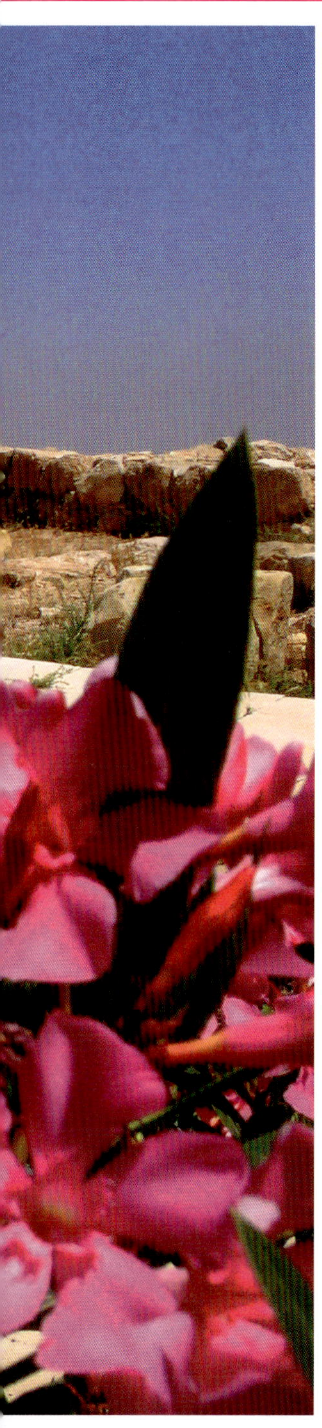

The ancient tradition of mosaic art is still practiced in Madaba, the 'capital city of mosaics'. Tiny pieces of colored limestone are intricately placed to create designs which are available in many boutiques.

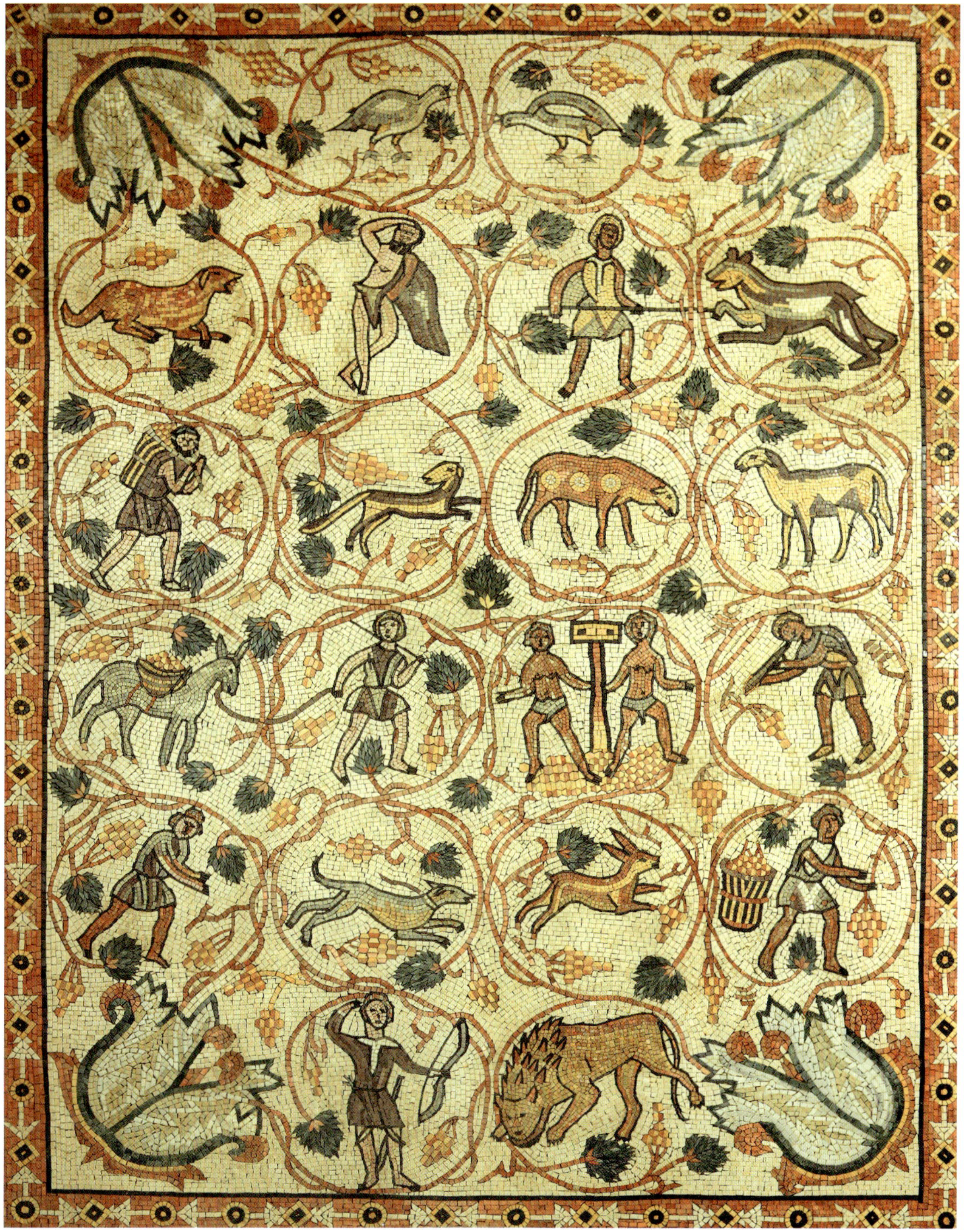

Moses Memorial Church sits high on the majestic Mount Nebo, overlooking the Holy Land. Moses is said to have died and been buried here.

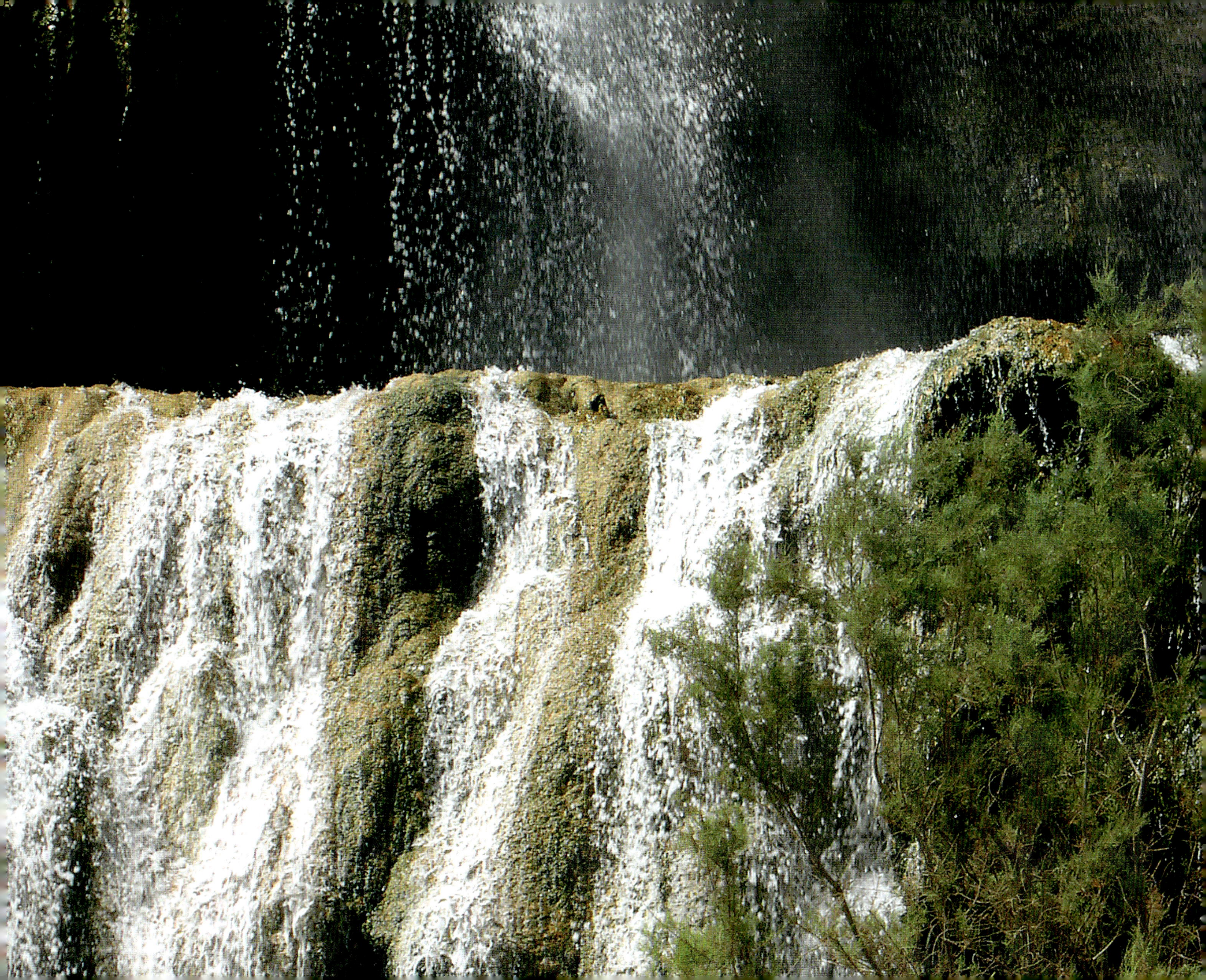

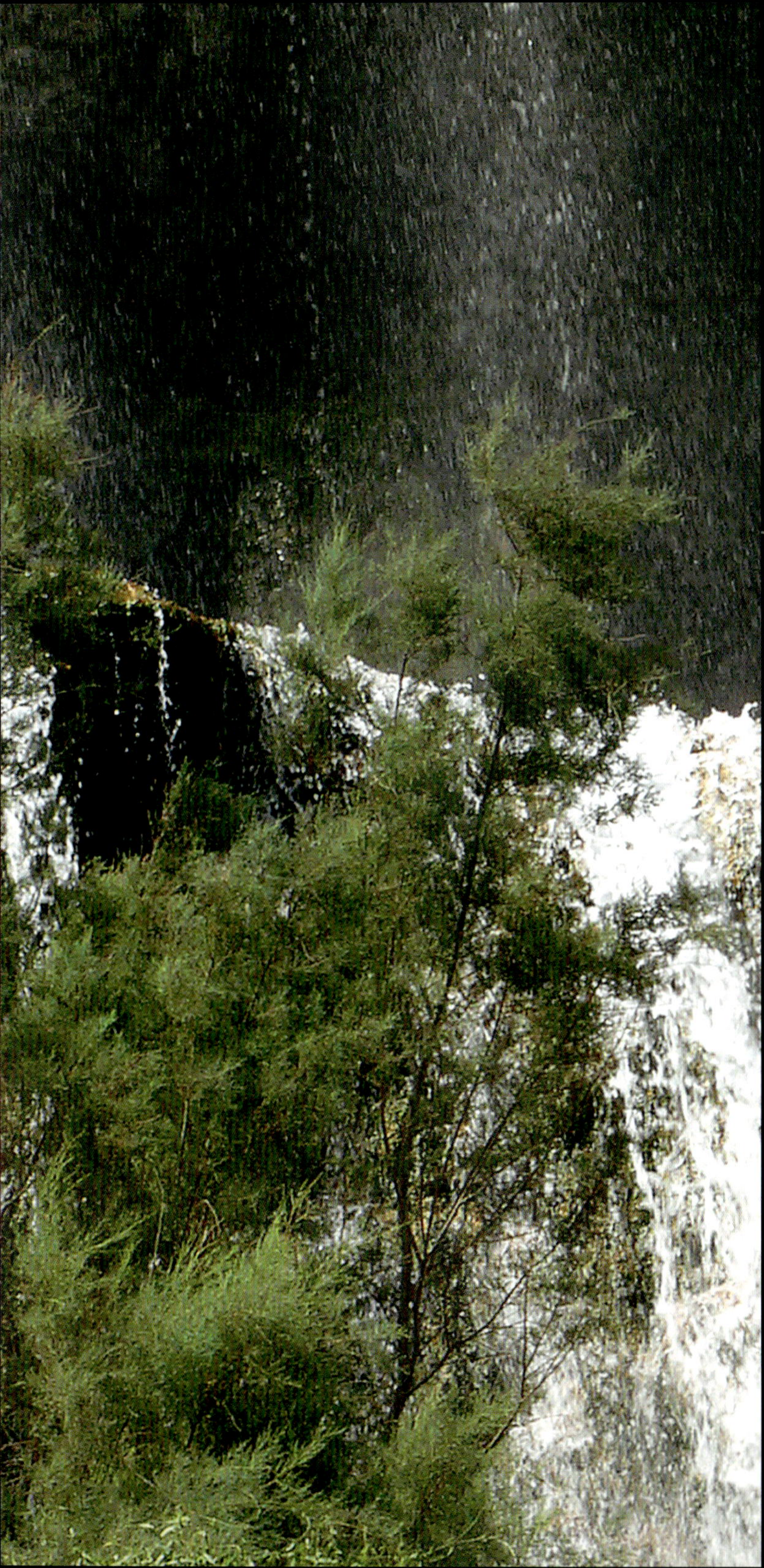

The waterfalls of Hammamat Ma'in appear like an oasis in an otherwise arid landscape, providing nourishment to desert flowers that bloom all year long. Fed by numerous thermal springs this site is a popular spa and bathing spot and is said to have provided healing powers since the days of King Herod.

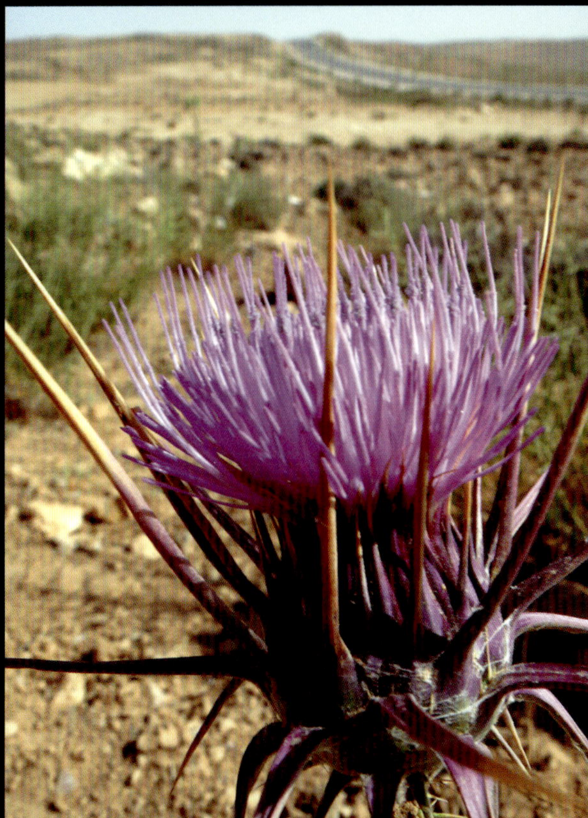

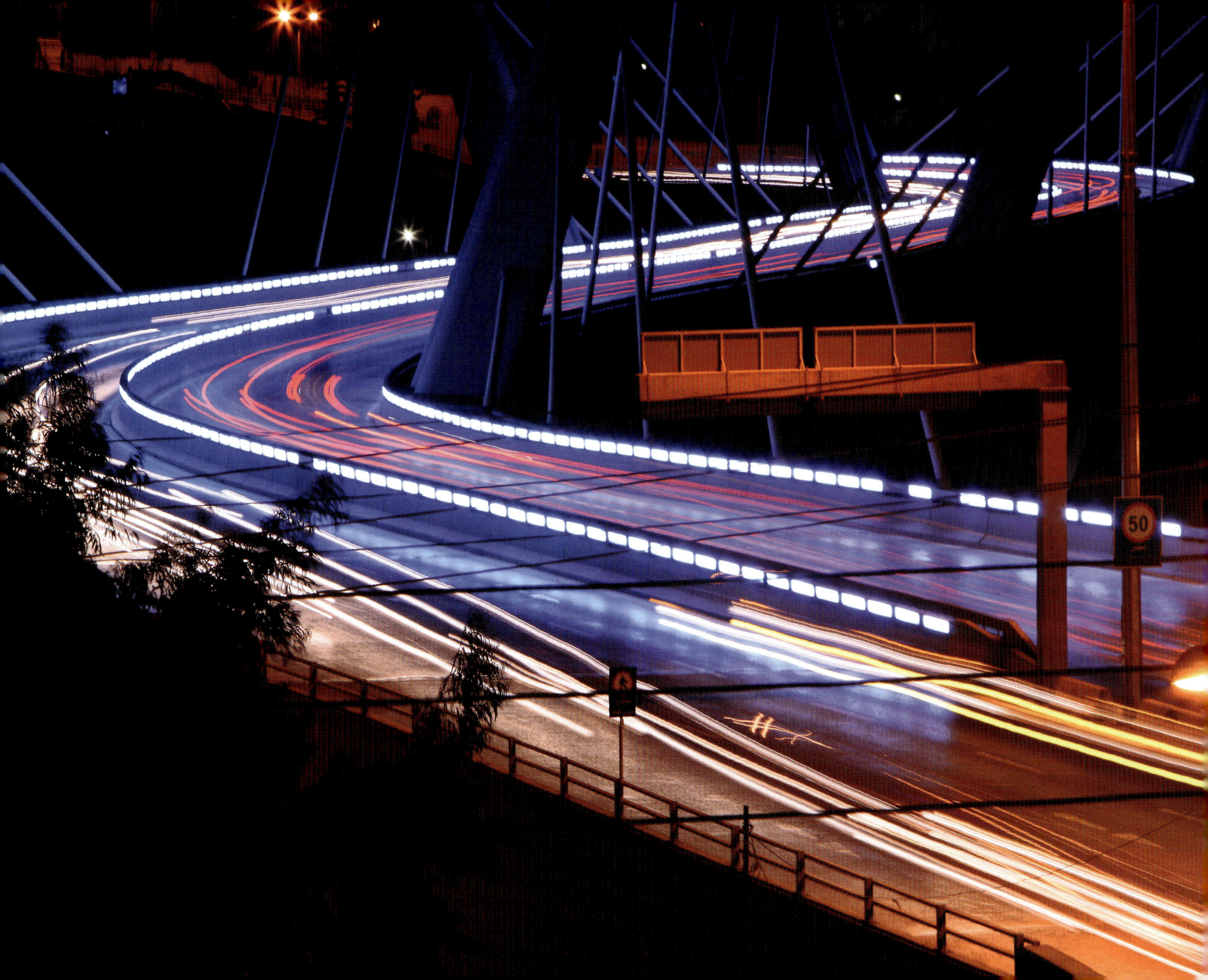
50

Cars create a serpent-like merge of light on the Abdoun Bridge. This first cable suspended bridge in Jordan connects the outskirts of the city with the popular nightlife area of Jabal Amman. Officially opened on December 14, 2006, it is 425 meters in length with a height of 45 meters above the valley floor.

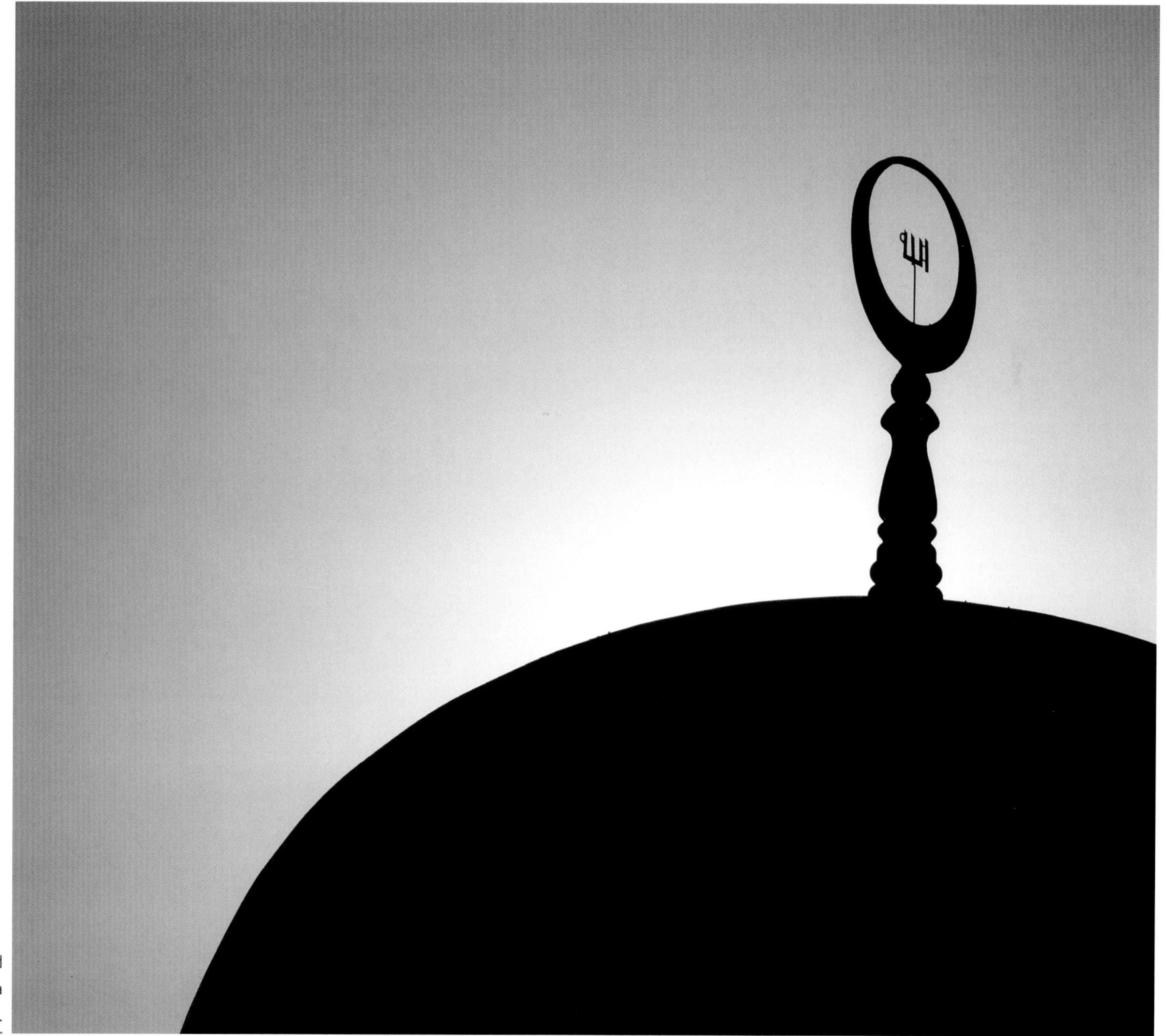

Allah – the Muslim word for God – is inscribed within the ring of a mosque's dome in Amman.

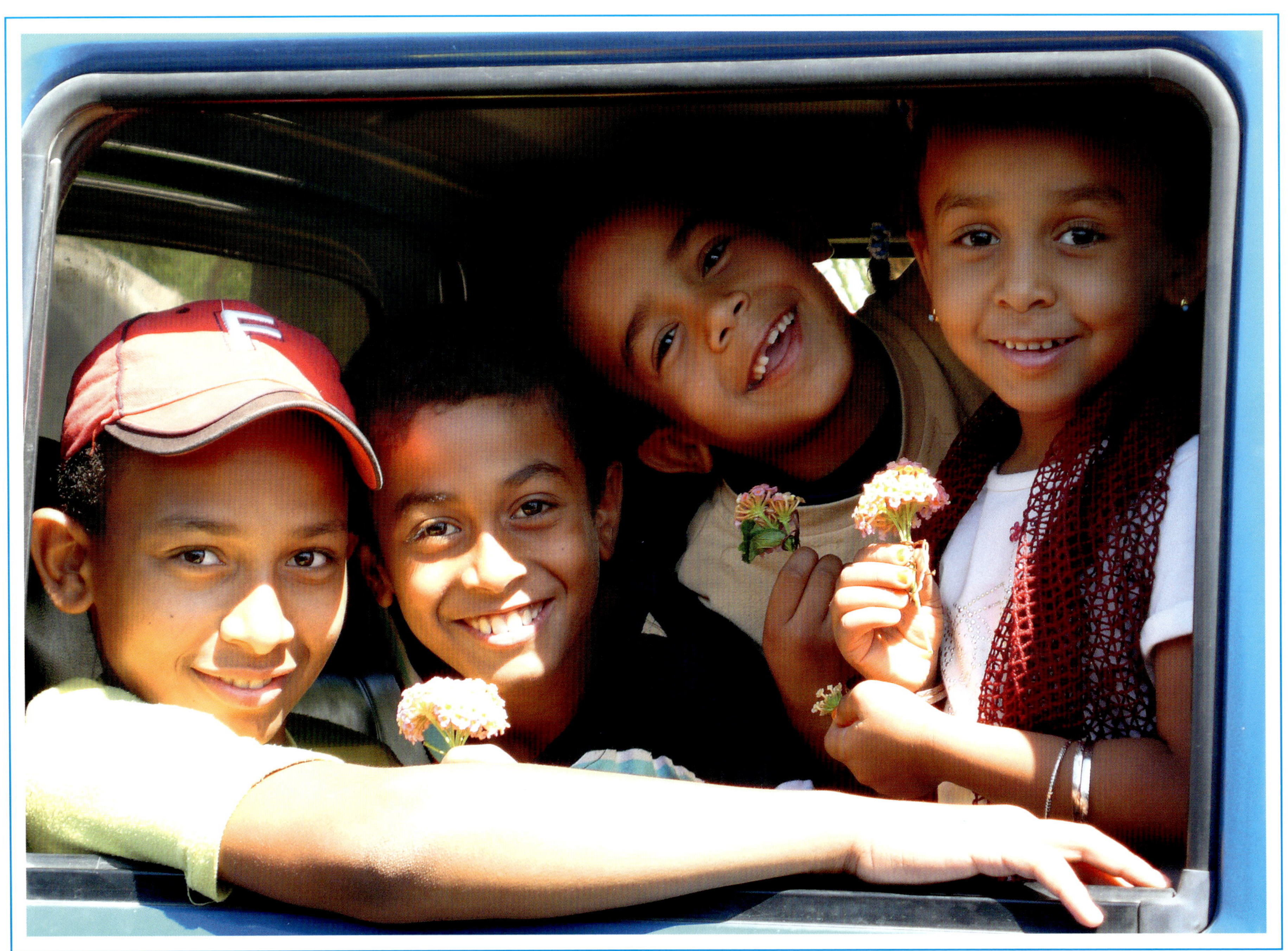

Happy faces peer out during a family ride on the Kings' Highway, which connects Amman and the seaside beach resort of Aqaba. A good reason to smile!

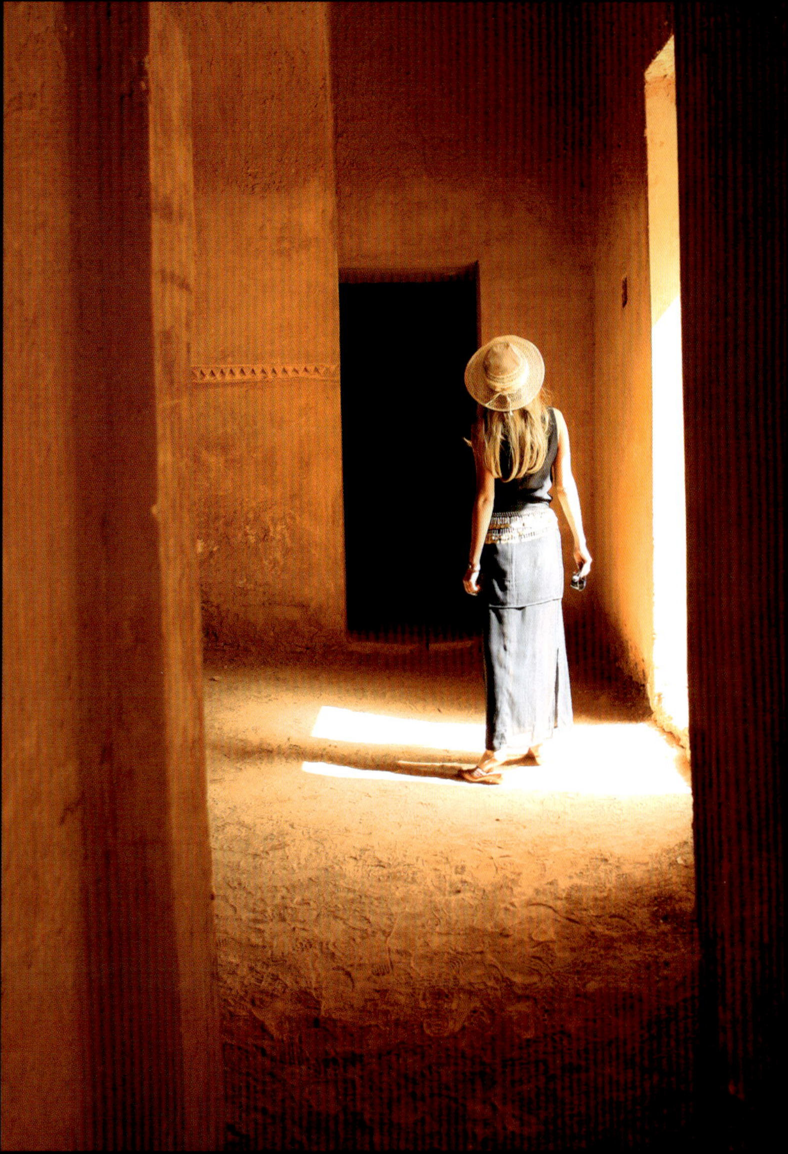

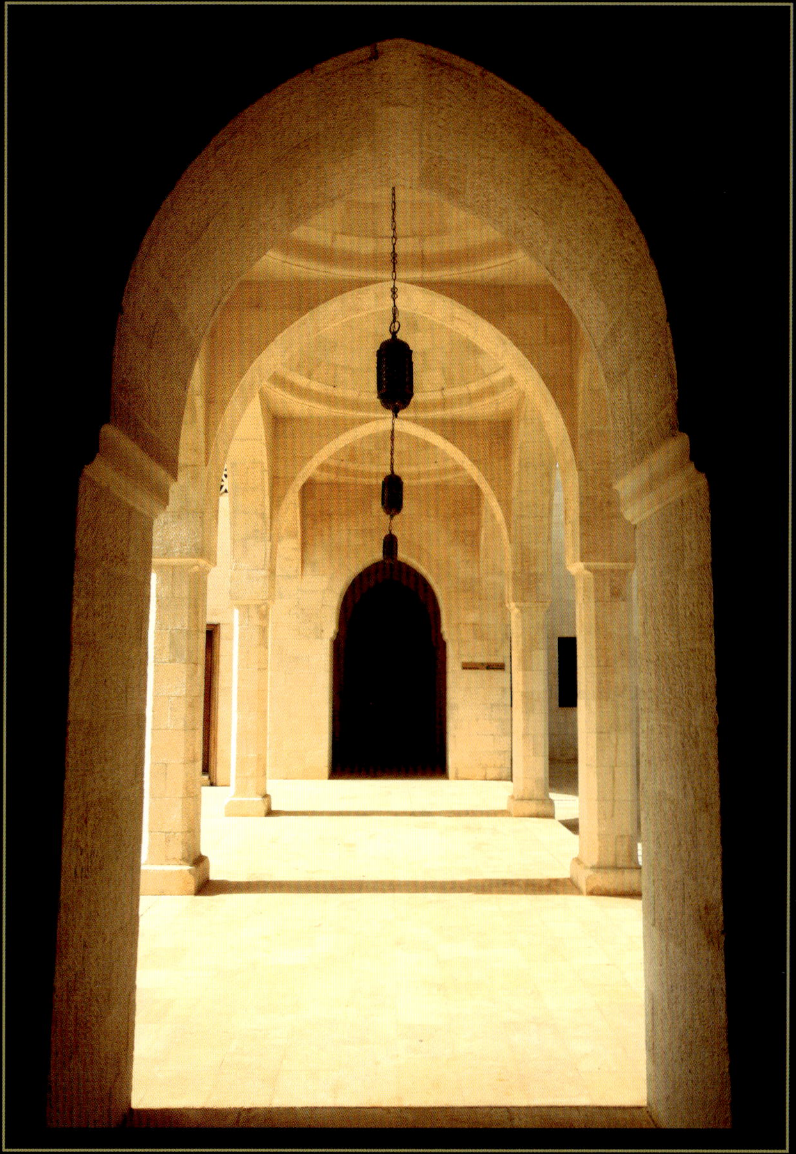

Shadow and light play on the walls of the Qasr al-Kharaneh – a fortress like desert castle that towers over the region and can be seen for miles from

Intricate arches within the courtyard of the Prophet Shoaibs Mosque.

The towering columns of the Temple of Hercules, built by Emperor Marcus Aurelius, has guarded this hillside of Amman known as Jabal al-Qal'ah (the Citadel) since AD161.

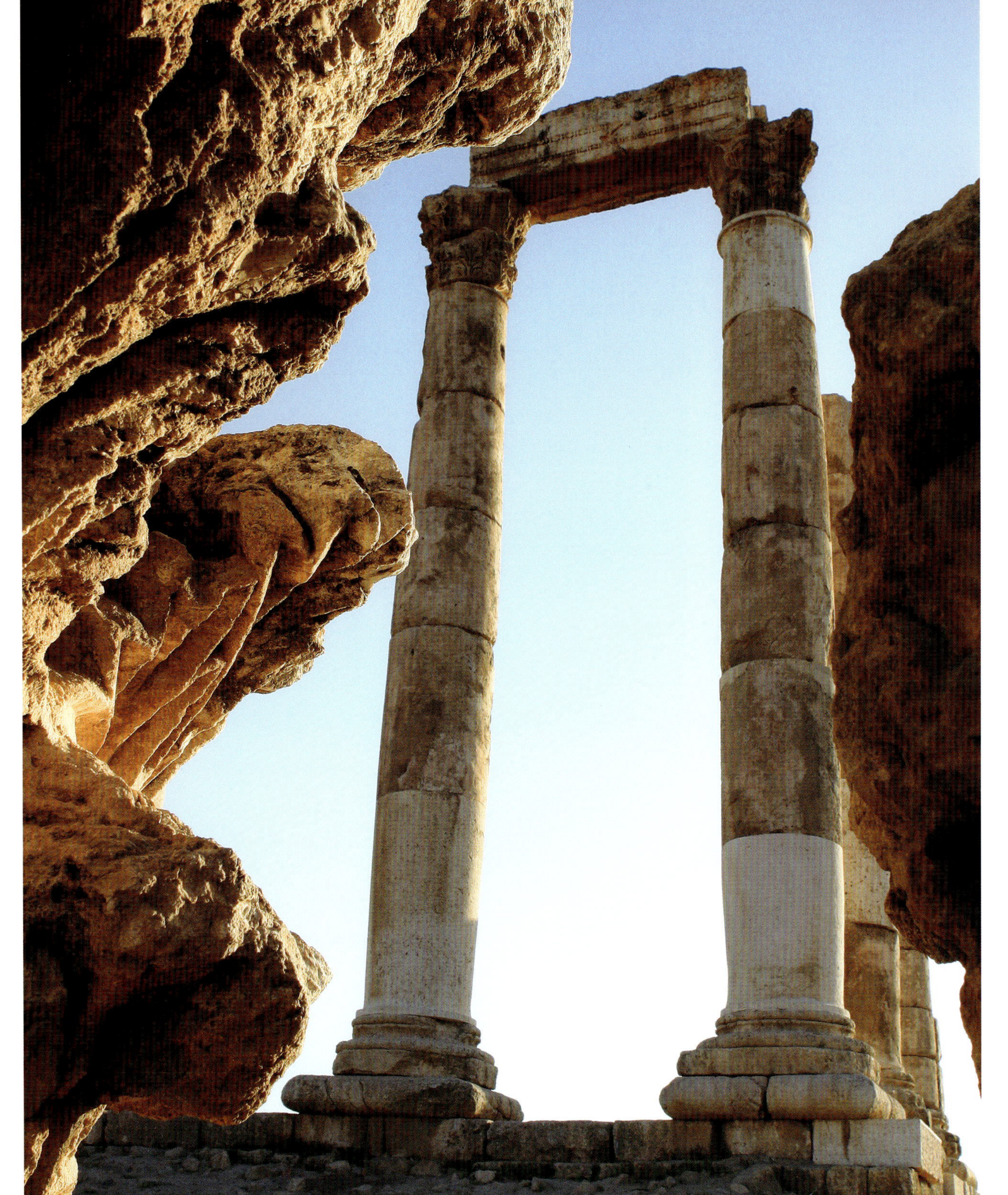

Enjoying a refreshing sea breeze in Tala Bay, the modern resort complex of hotels and private residences on the shores of the Red Sea in Aqaba.

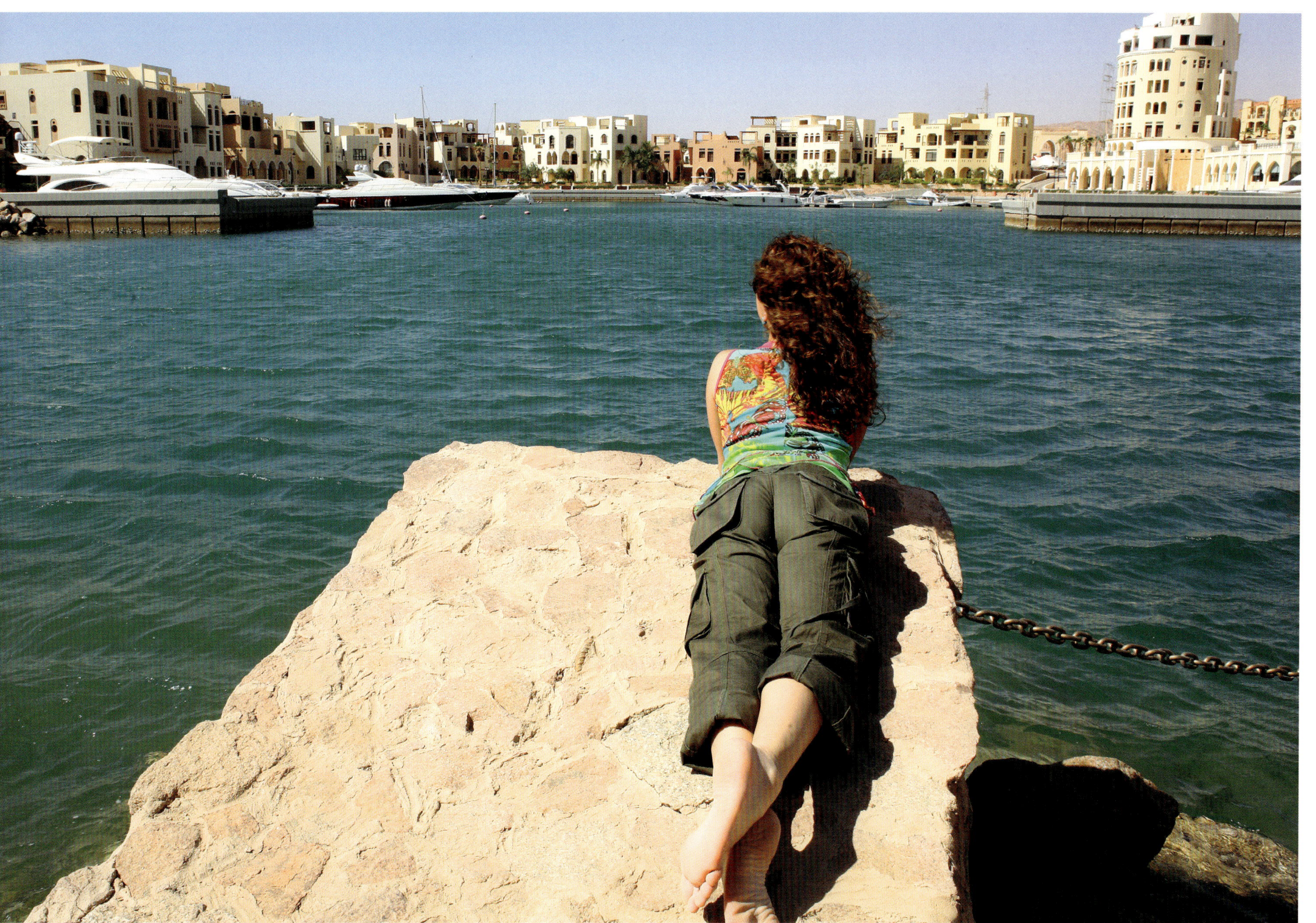

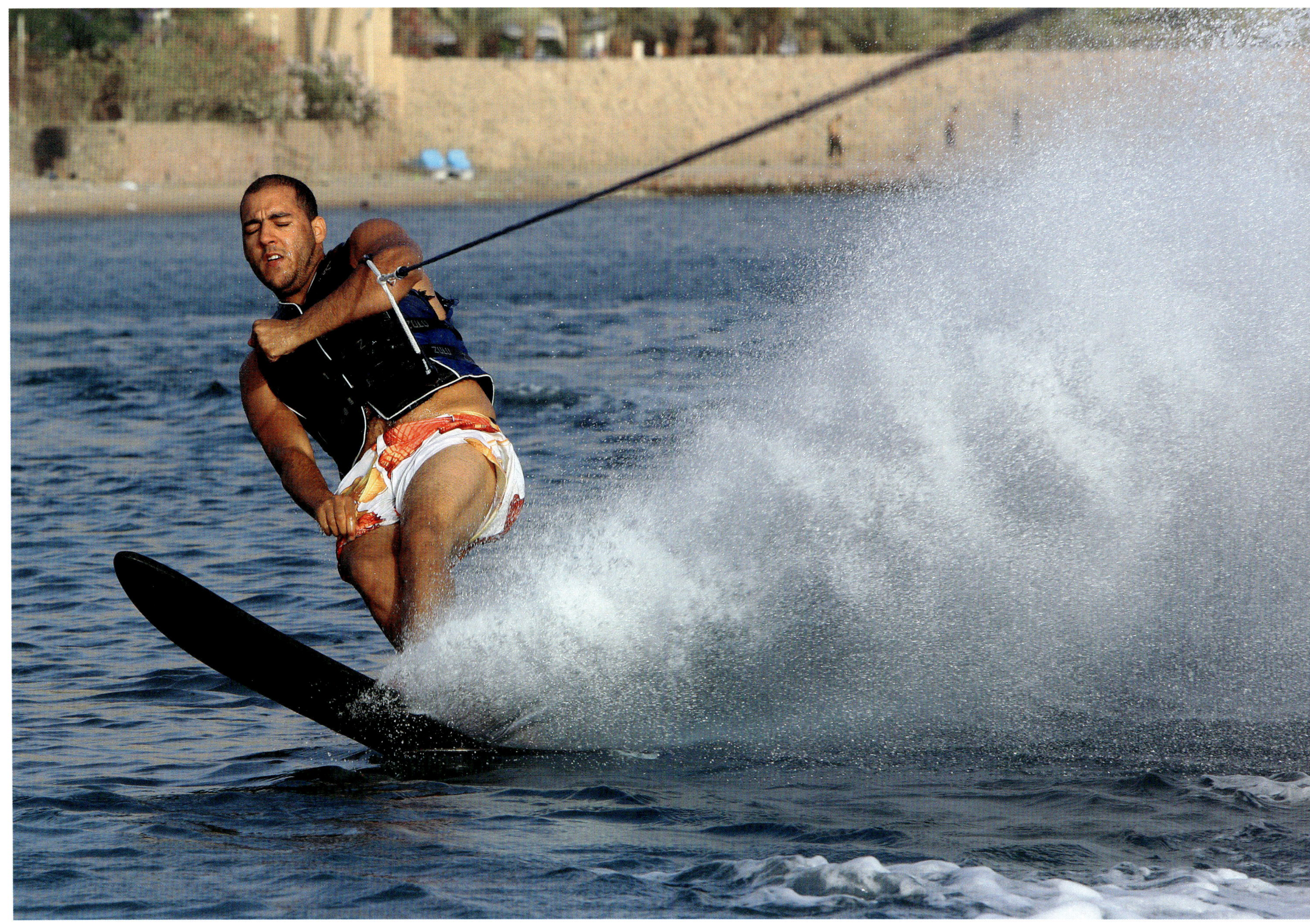

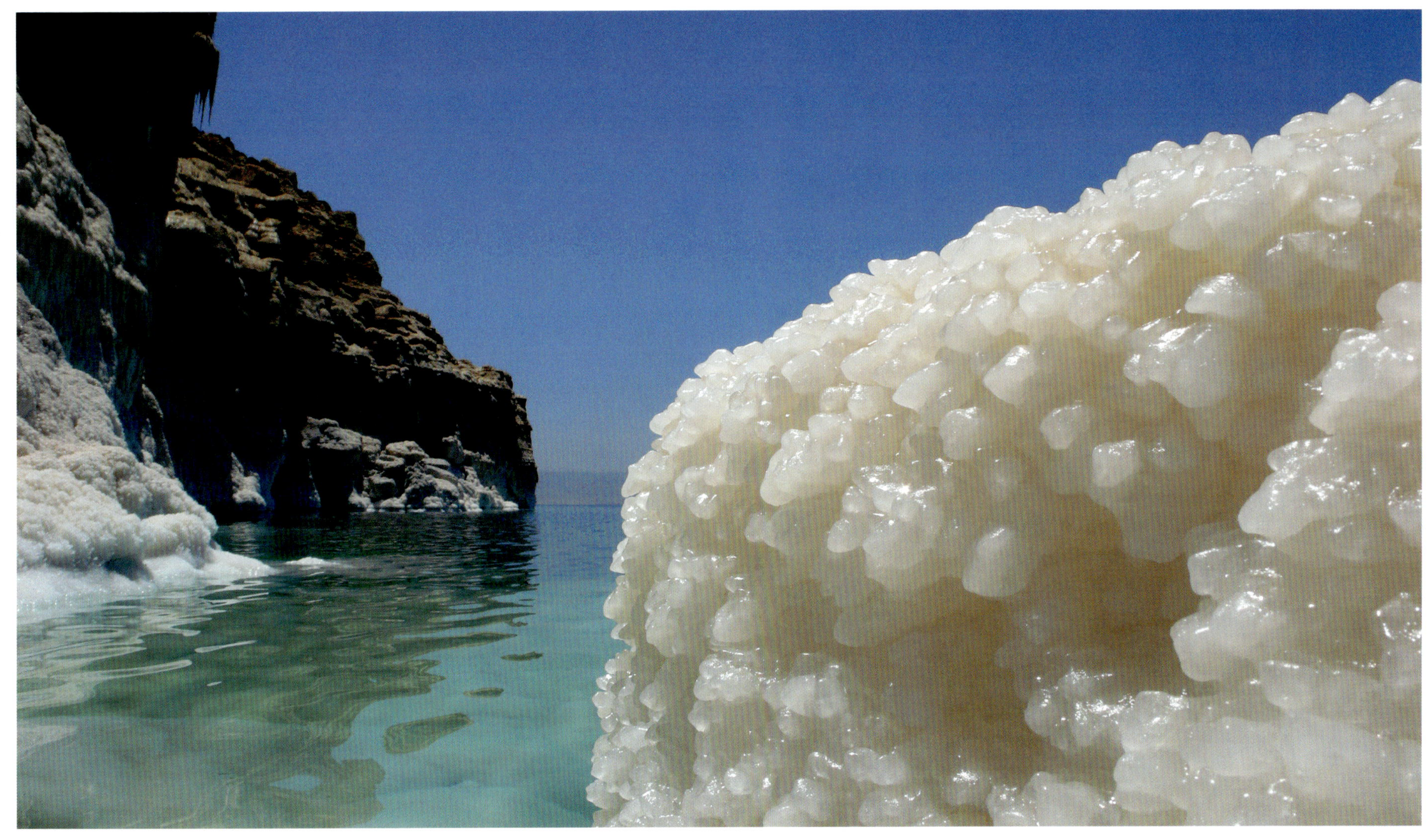

Dive, snorkel, waterski or just relax and unwind on shore at the only beach resort in Aqaba, situated at the southern tip of Jordan.

The Dead Sea, famed as the lowest point on earth, offers crystalline formations and salt domes that sparkle brilliantly in the blue waters.

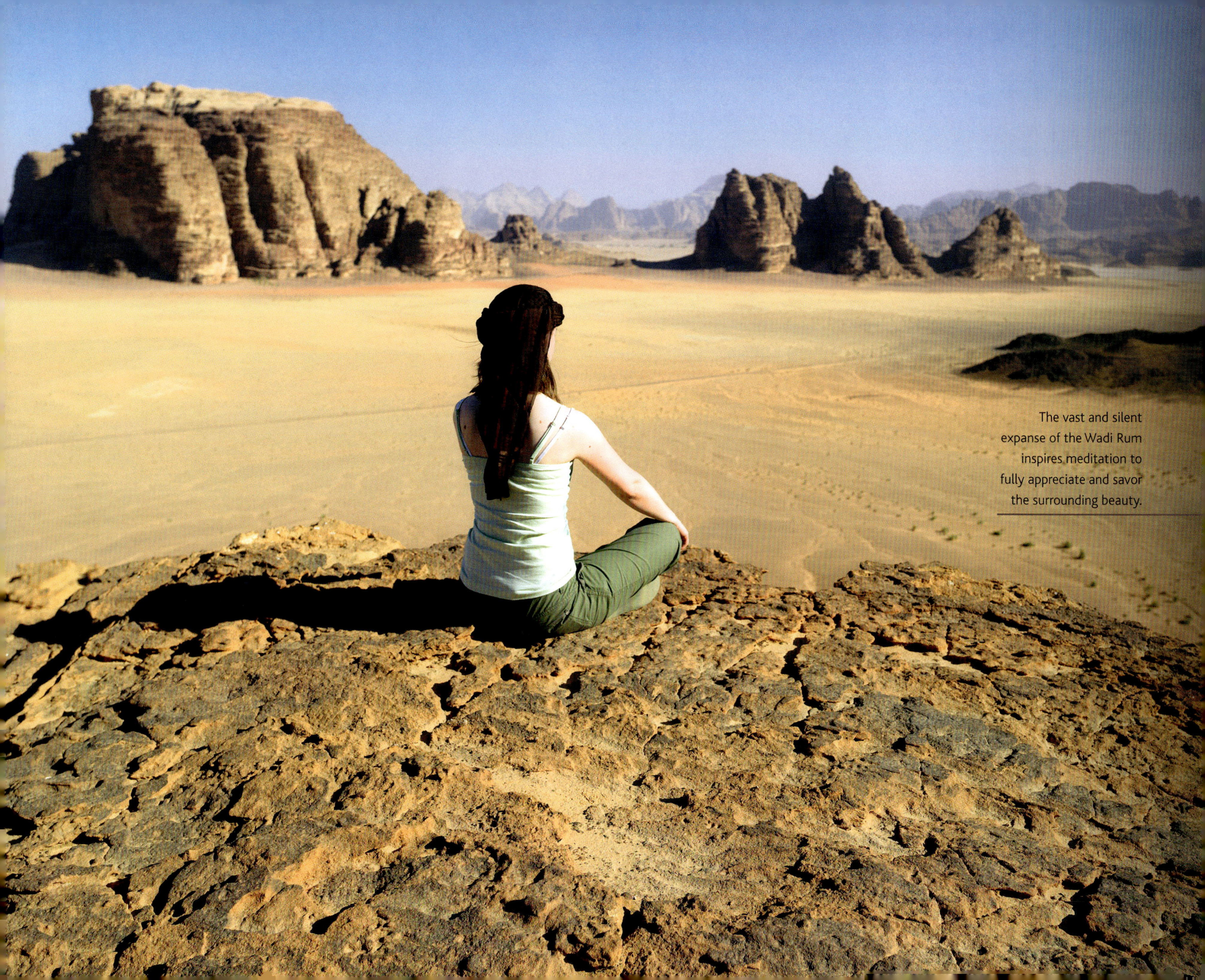

The vast and silent expanse of the Wadi Rum inspires meditation to fully appreciate and savor the surrounding beauty.

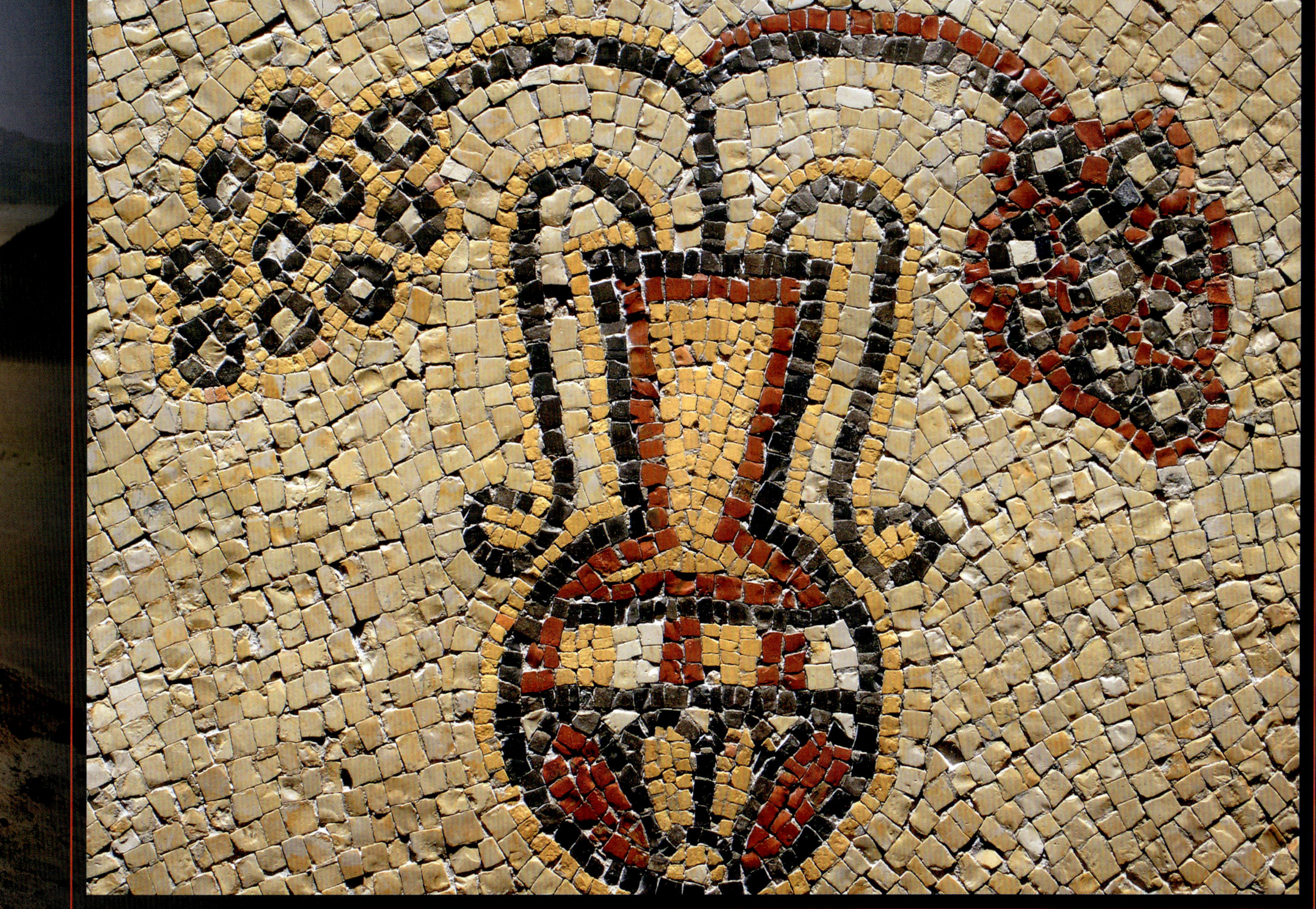

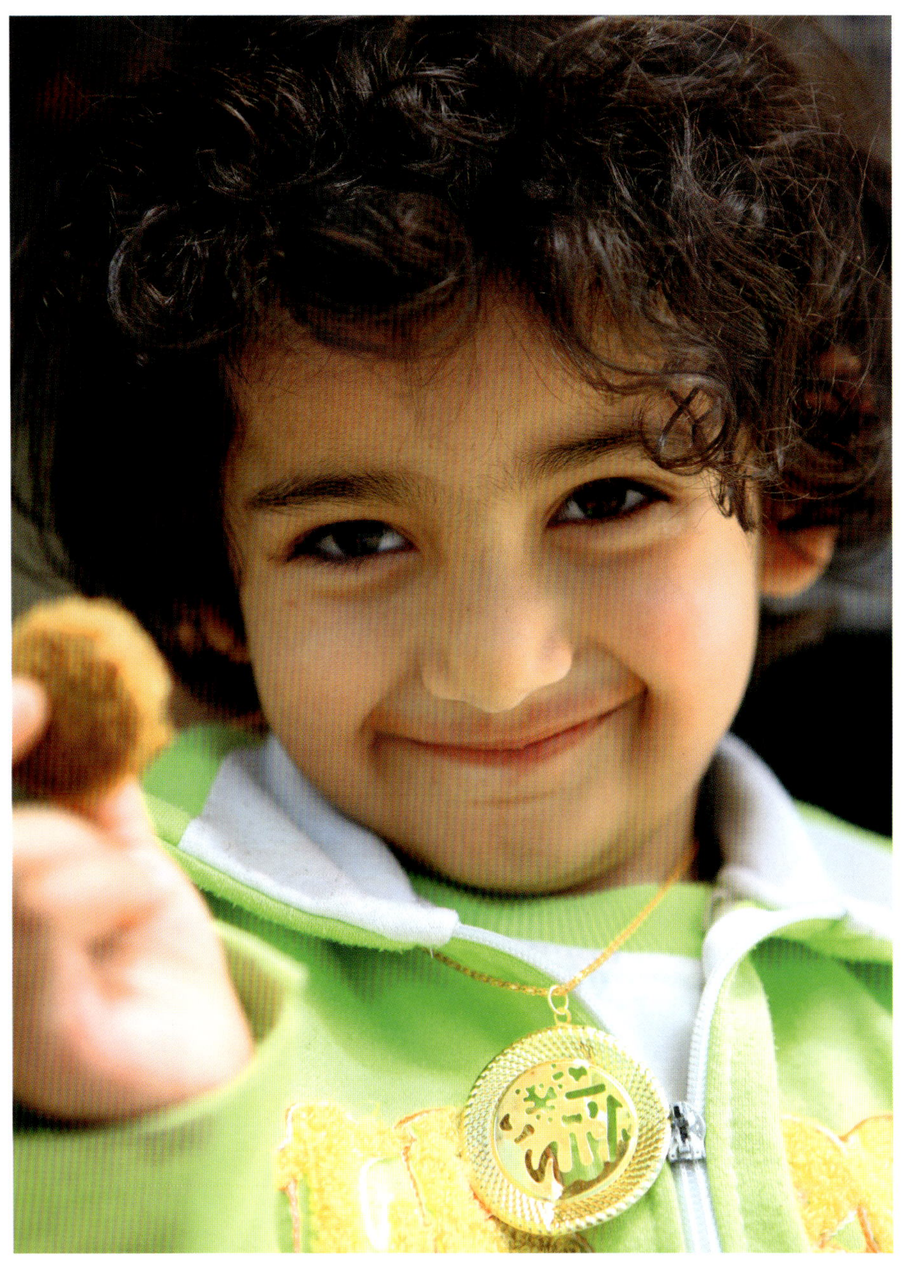

An innocent child's smile at a market in Amman, followed by an offer to share are frequent expressions of warmth and hospitality displayed throughout the country.

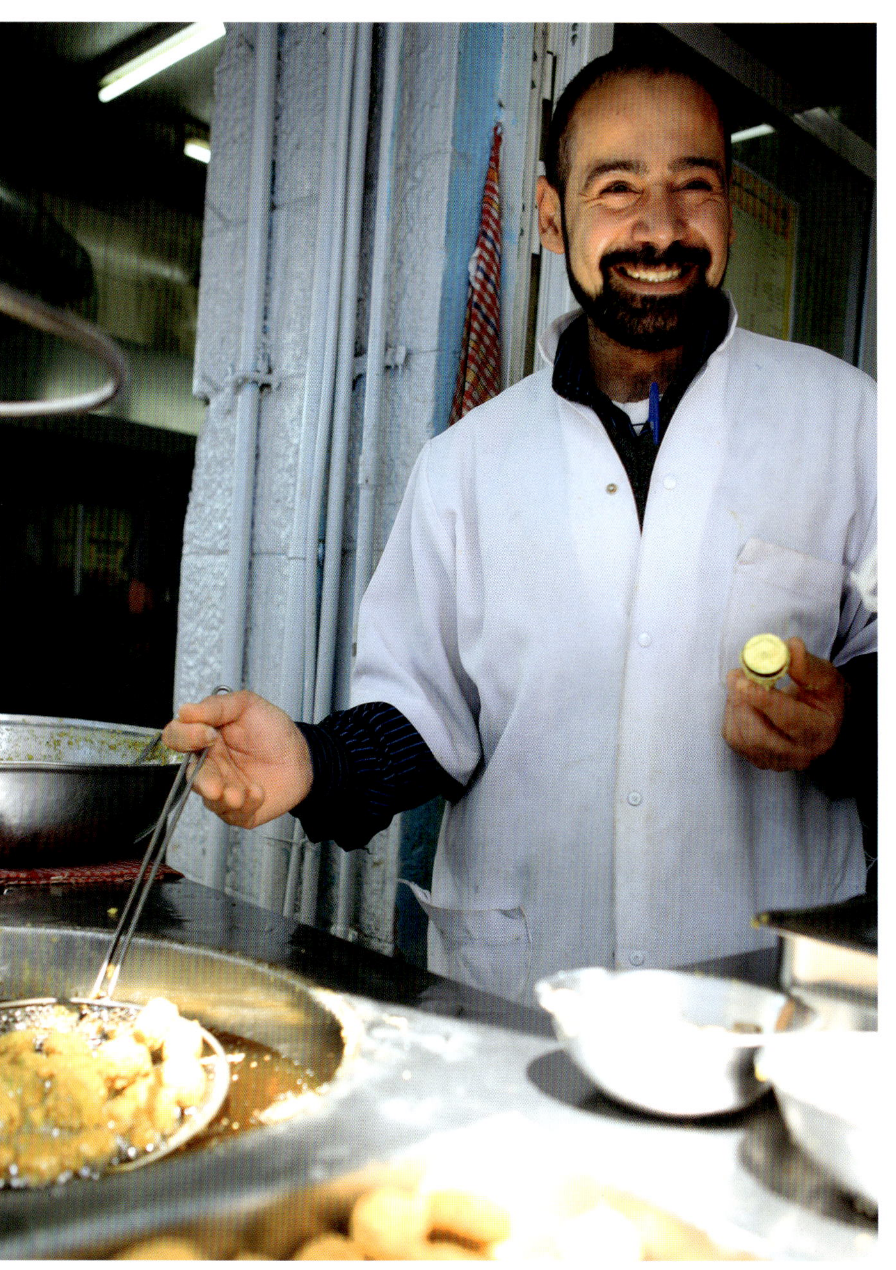

In the souq (market) of Amman, the pungent, sweet aroma of local spices, herbs and seeds, entice the sense of smell.

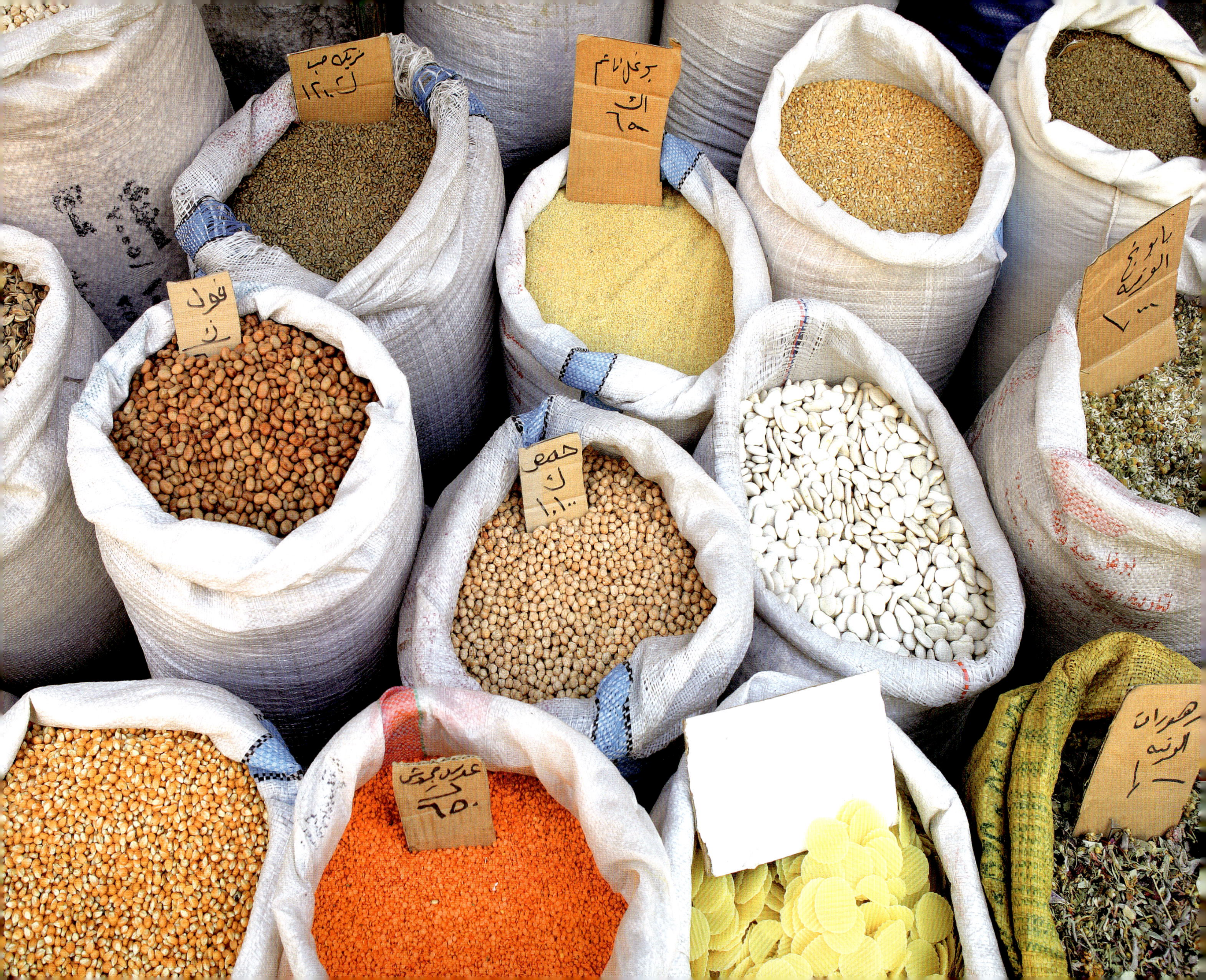
فول
حمص

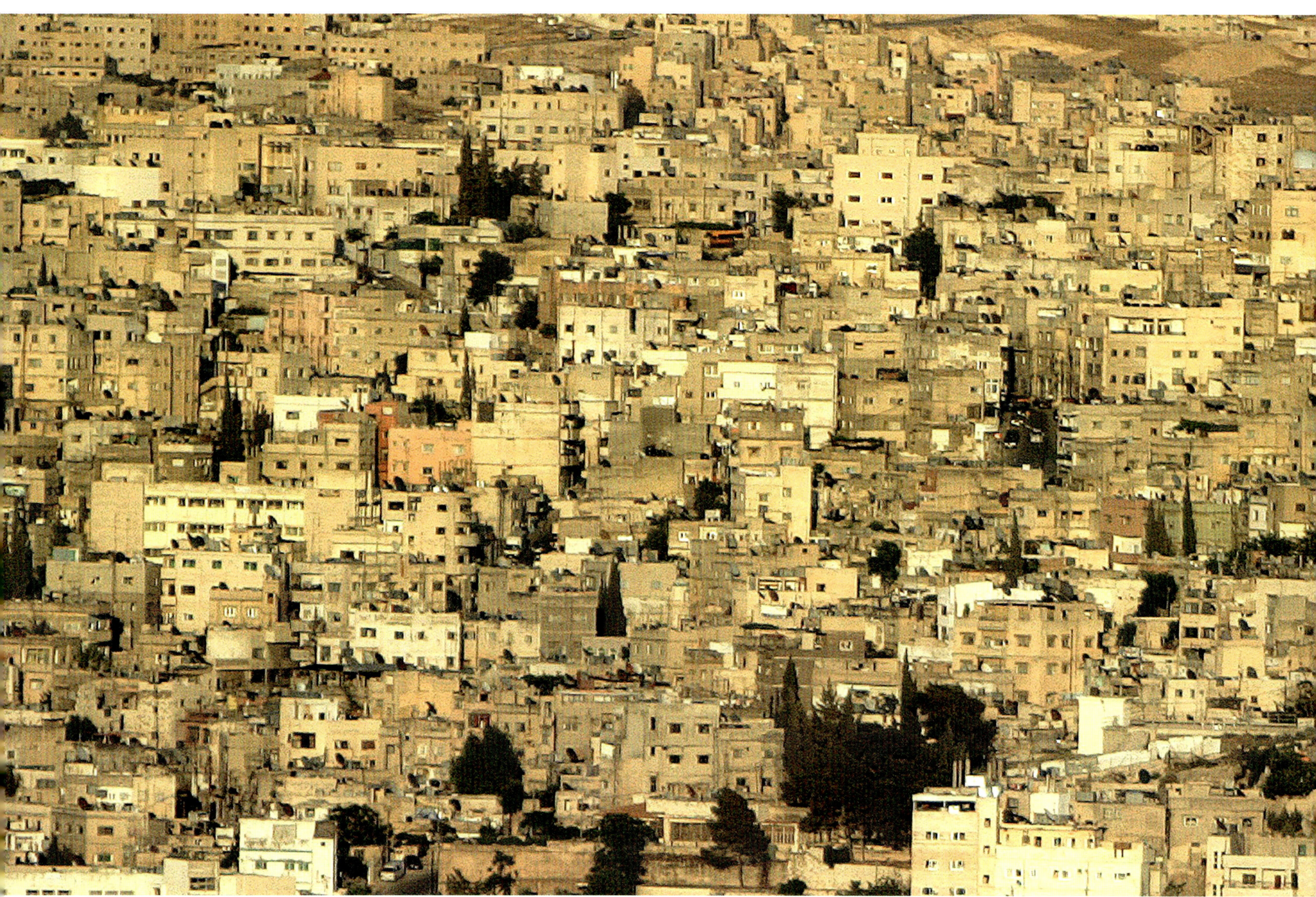

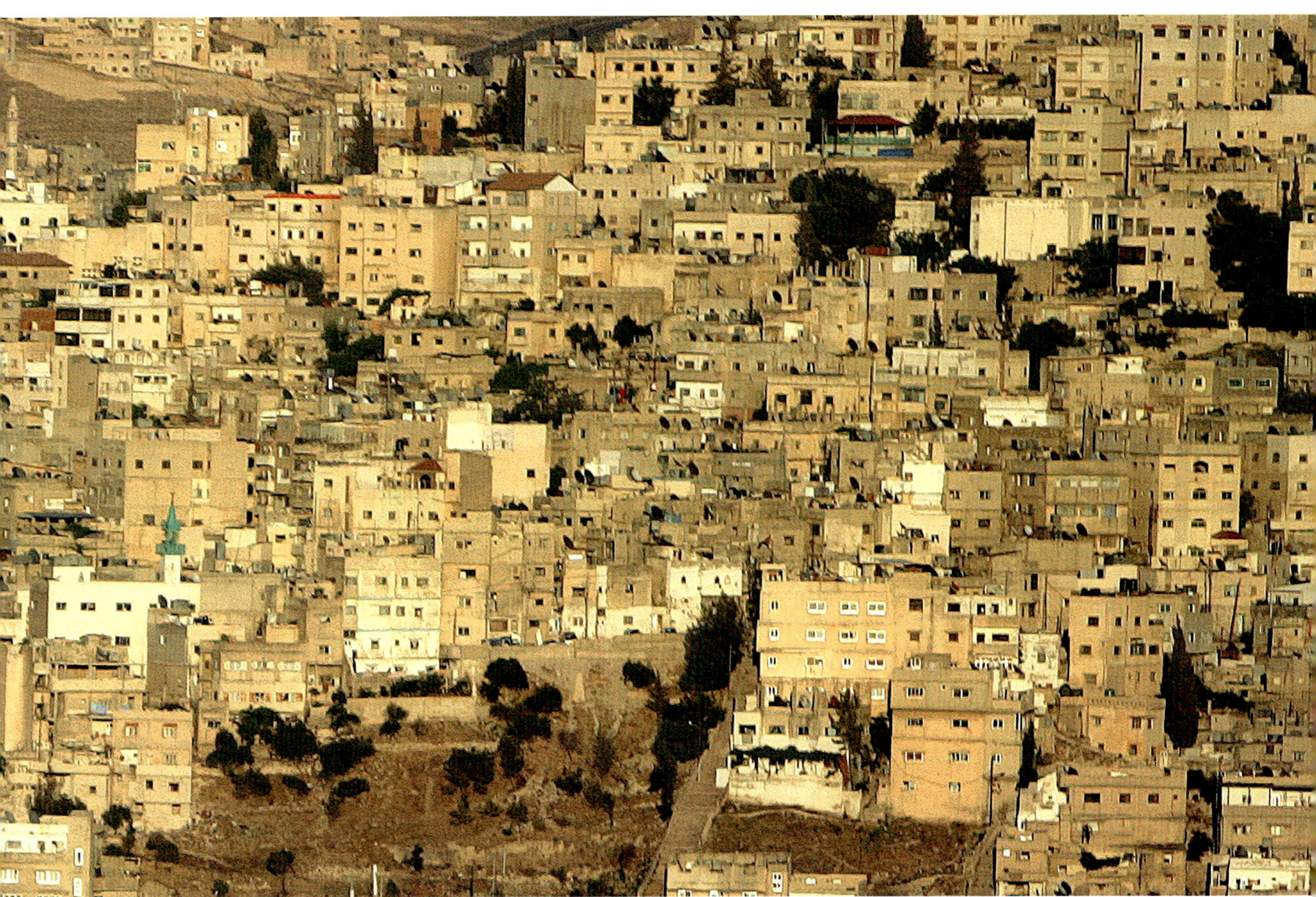

A golden sunset bathes the Jordanian capital of Amman in pastel hues.

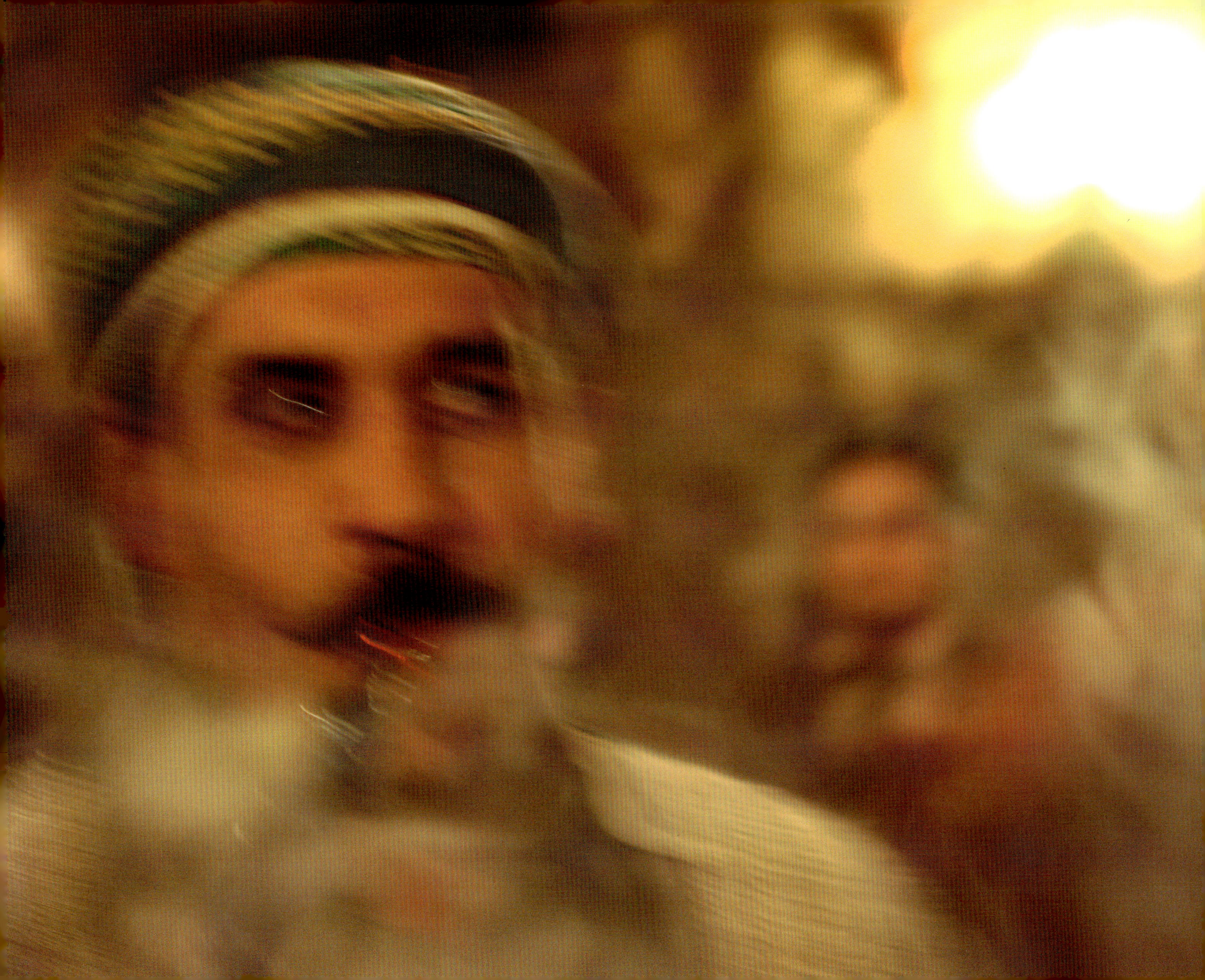

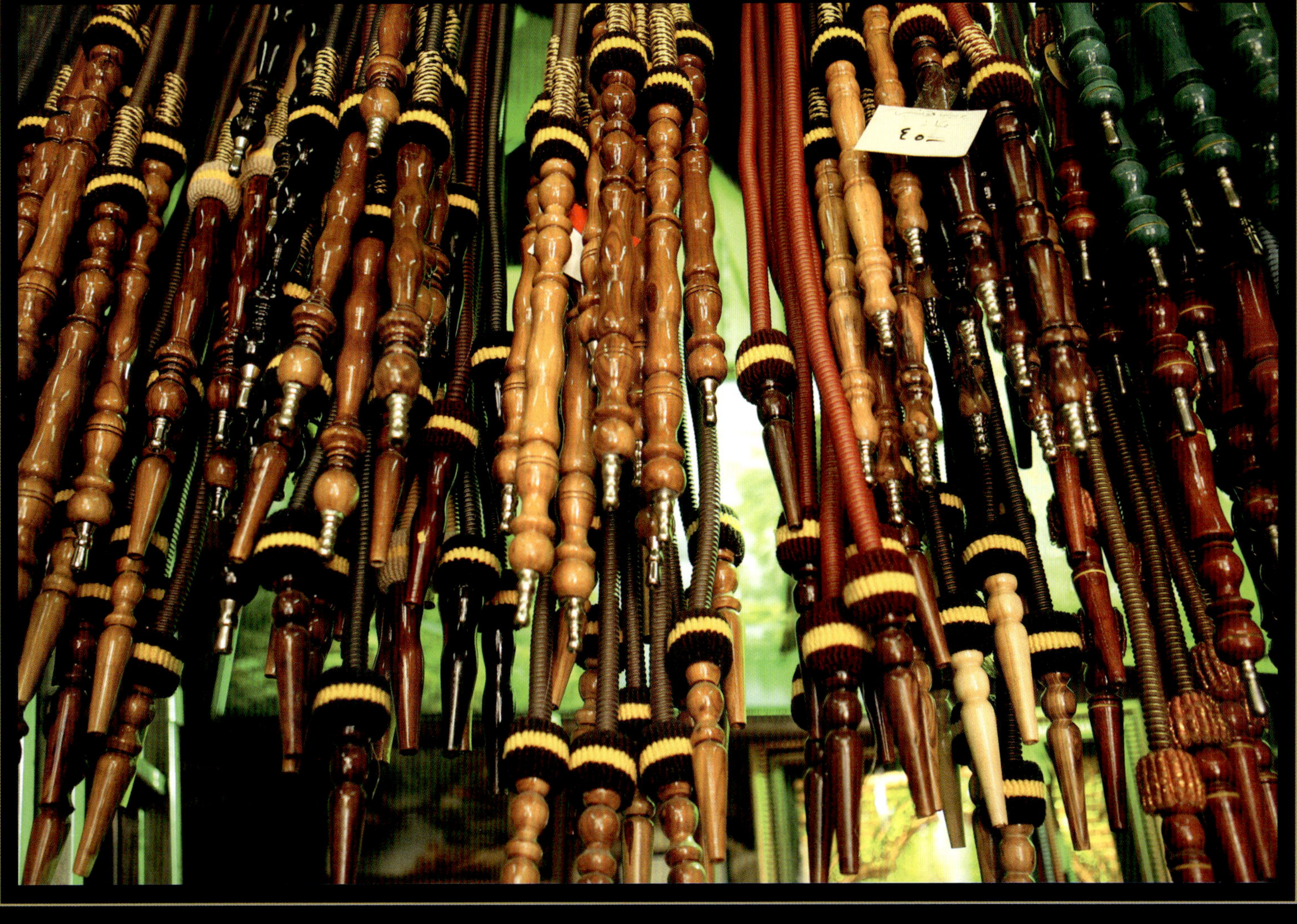

Egyptians call it *Shisha*; Lebanese refer to it as *Nargile*; in English, it's *Hookah*. Jordanians call it *relaxation*. This ancient water pipe has been used for centuries to smoke away the day's stress while relaxing with friends and family. It is a favorite pastime, enjoyed in many cafés and restaurants throughout the country.

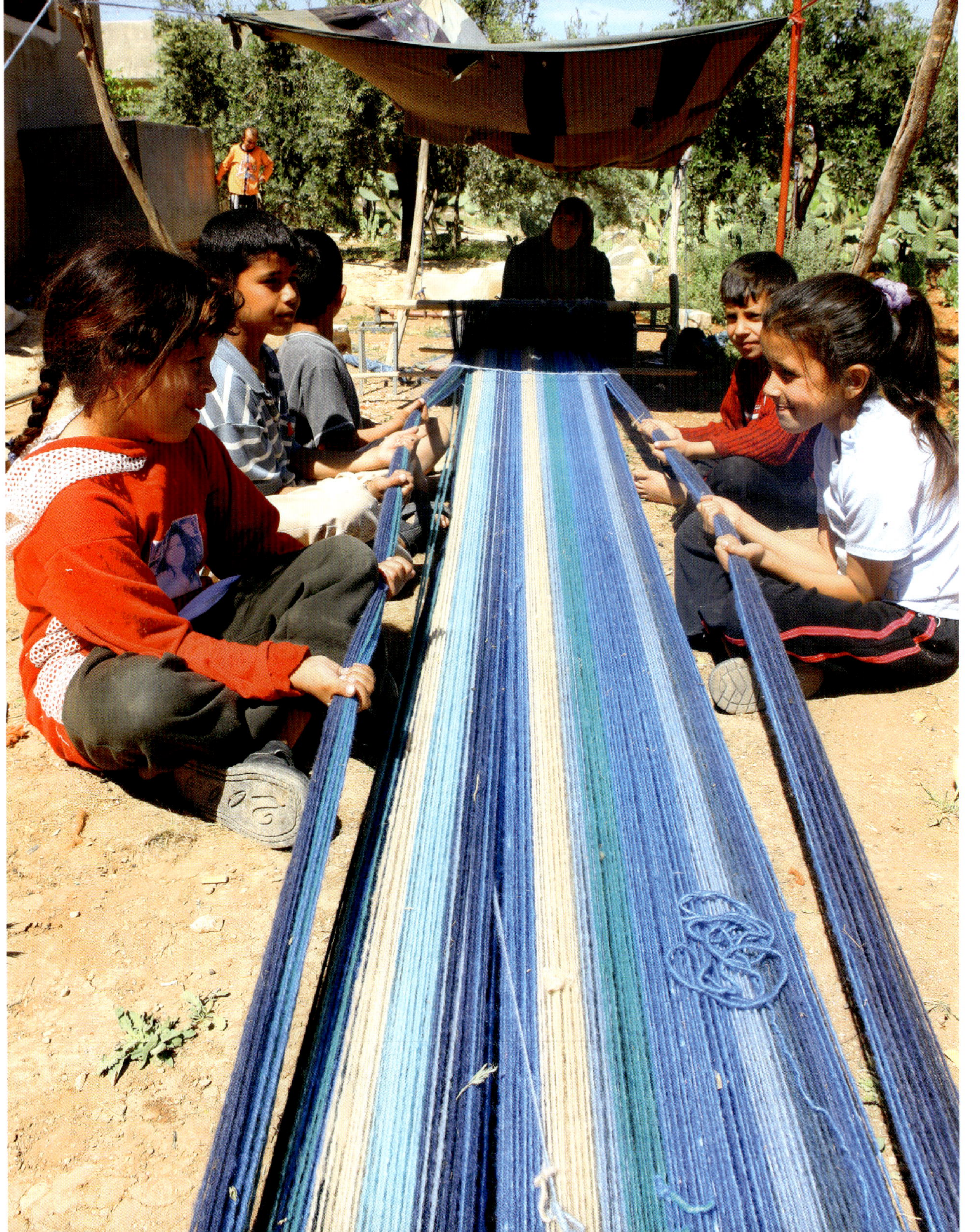

Lively fabrics are popular for their cheery, multicolored patterns.

In The Bani Hamida Women's Weaving Project near Mukawir (south of Madaba), one can watch local women weave colorful rugs on the traditional ground looms, constructed of stones, sticks and other available objects.

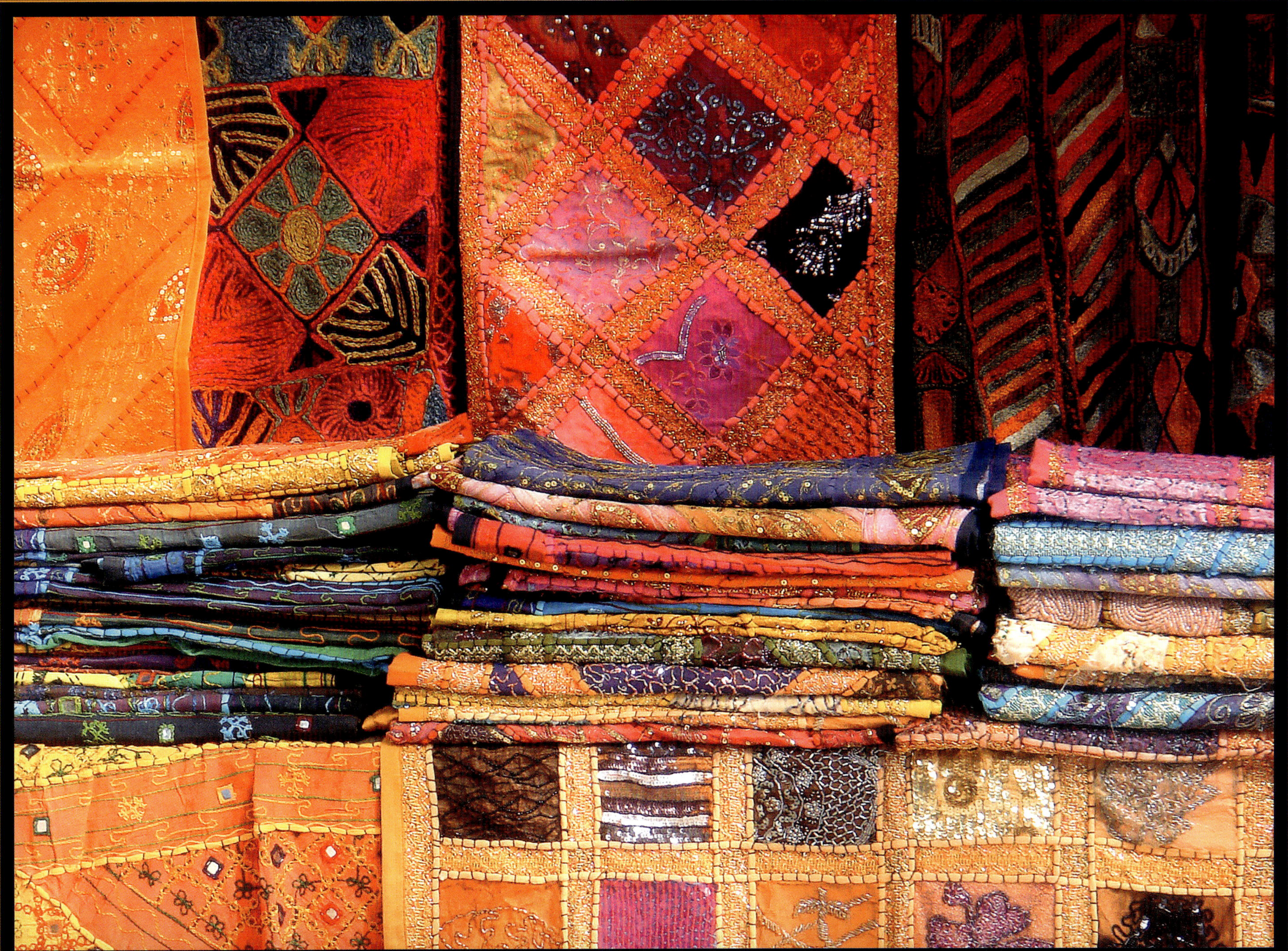

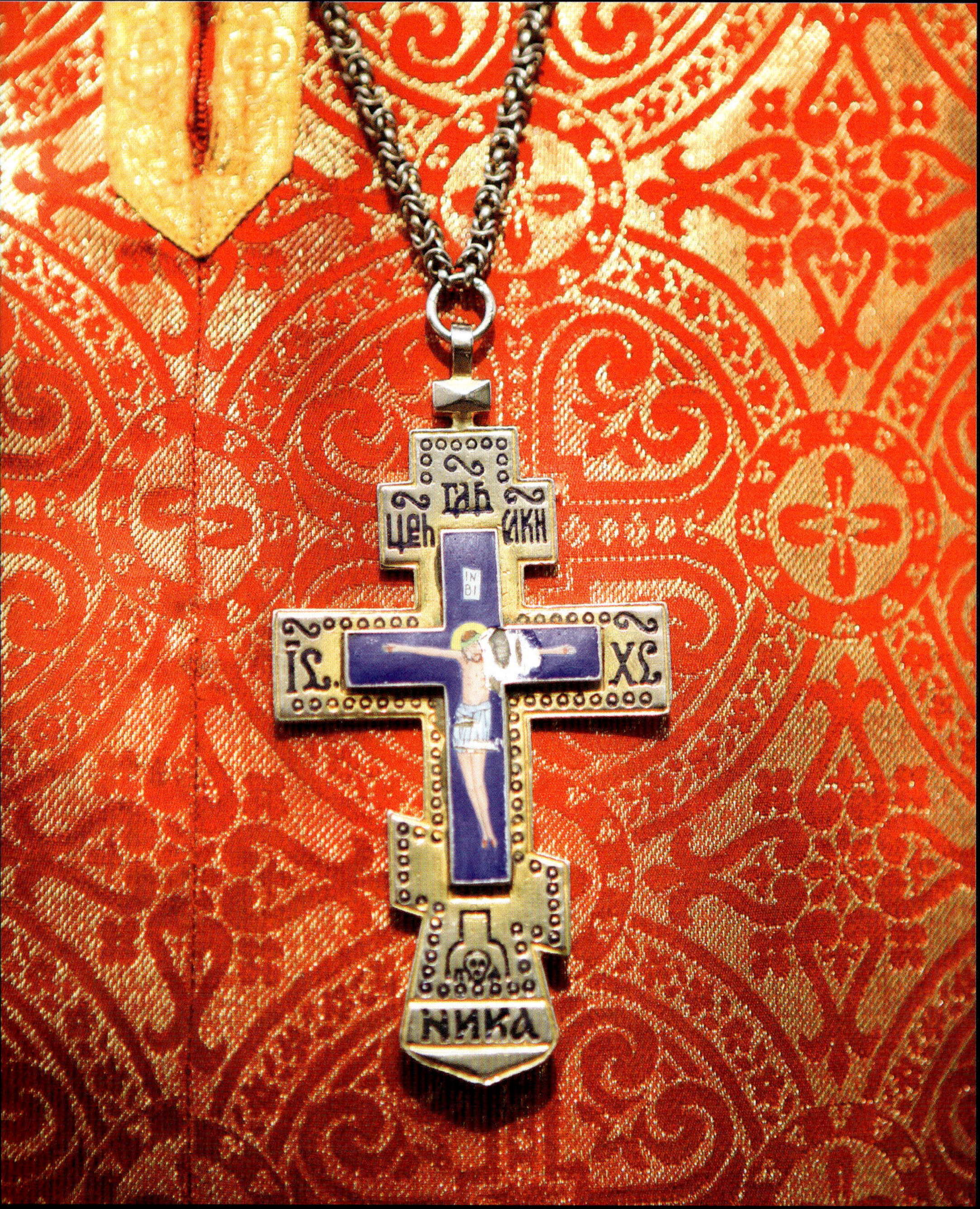

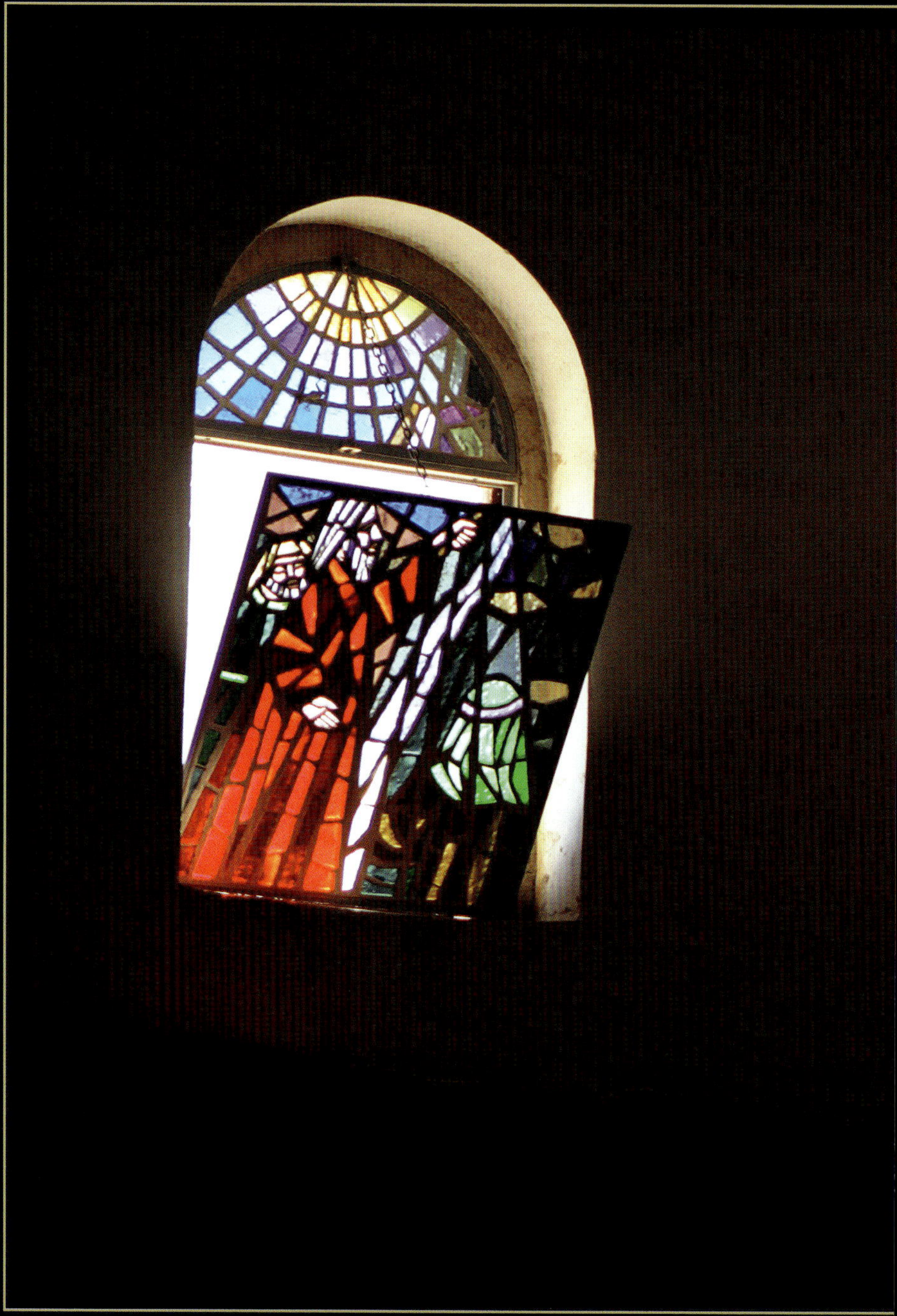

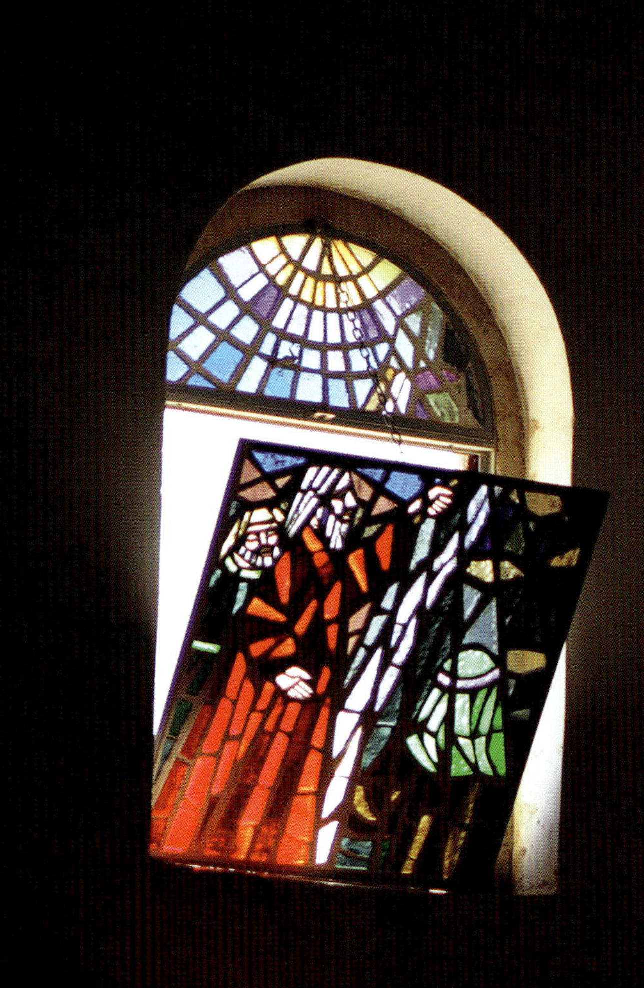

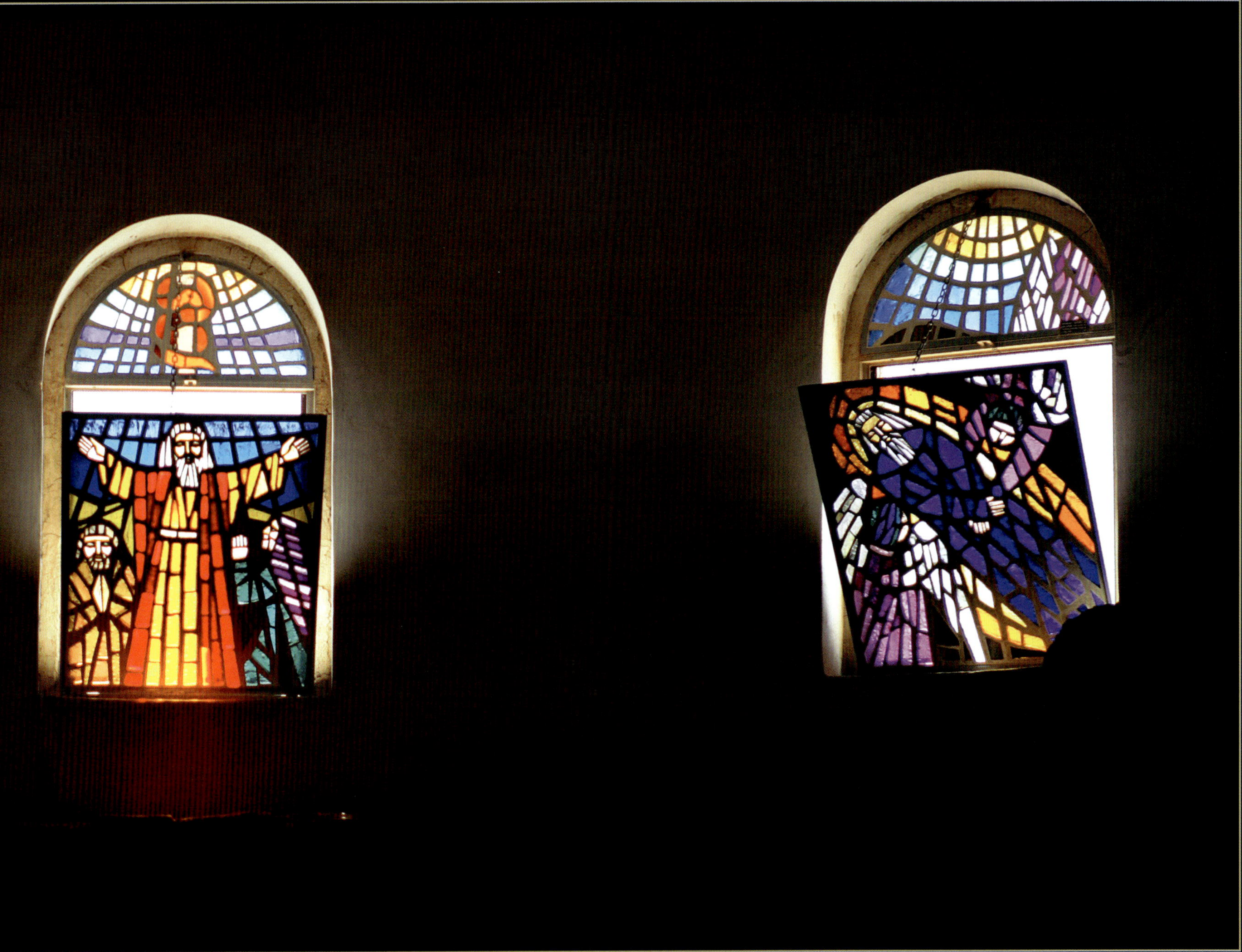

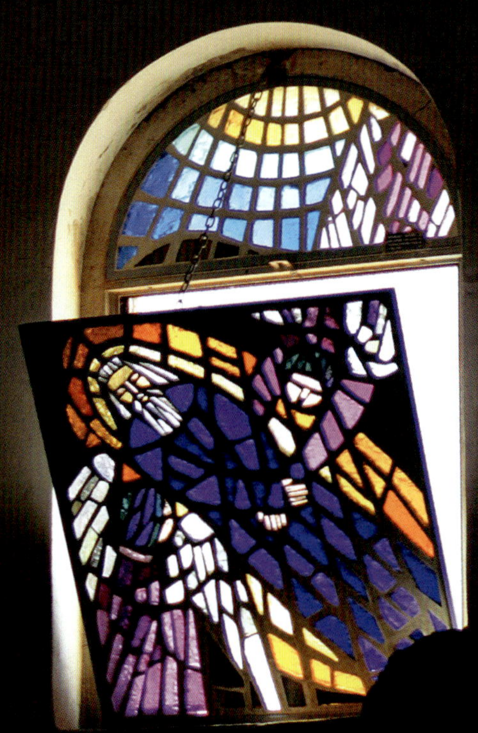

The stained glass windows of the Moses Memorial Church on Mount Nebo colorfully depict the figure of Moses, who is said to have been buried at the site. Pope John Paul II visited the Church in 2000.

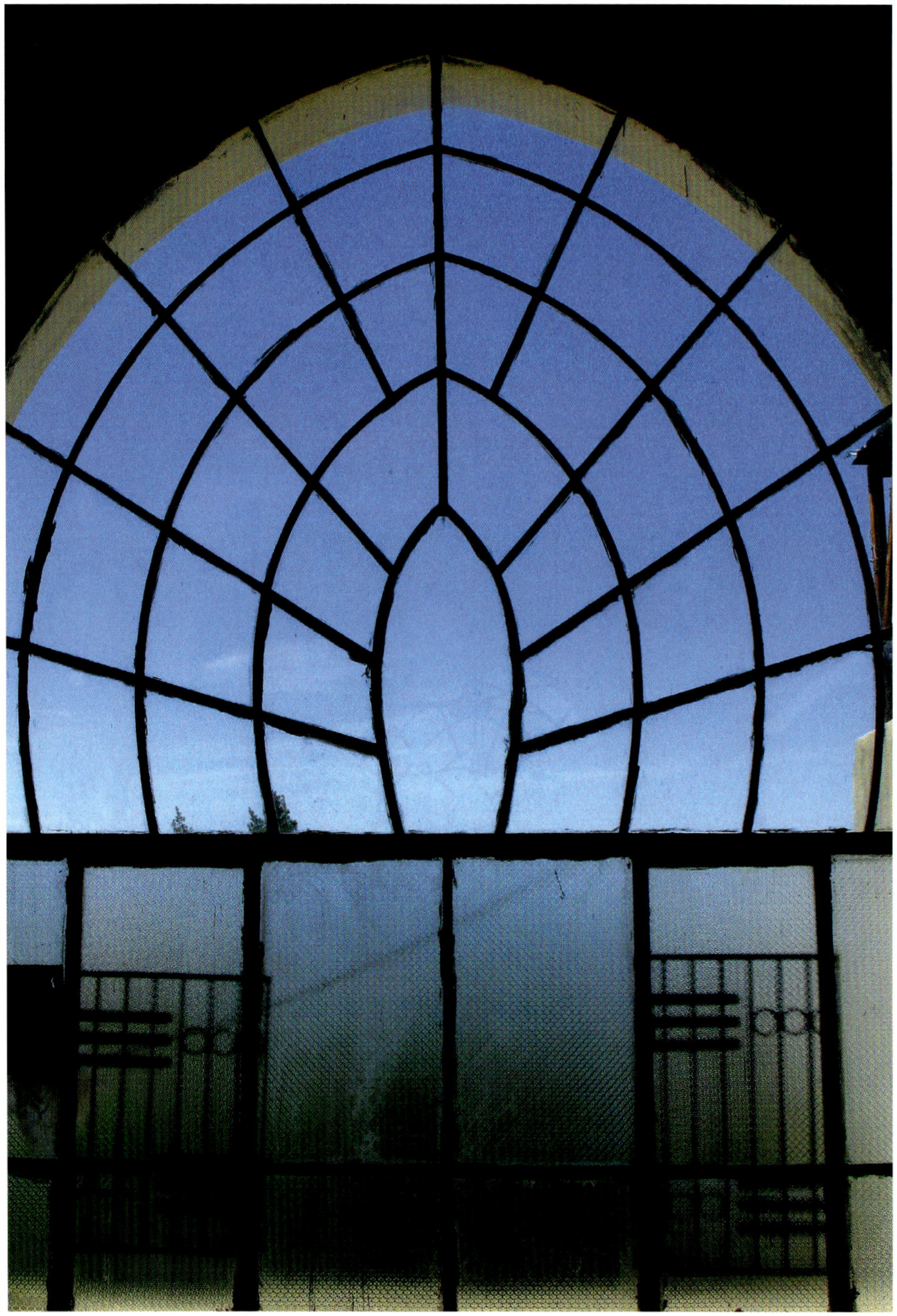

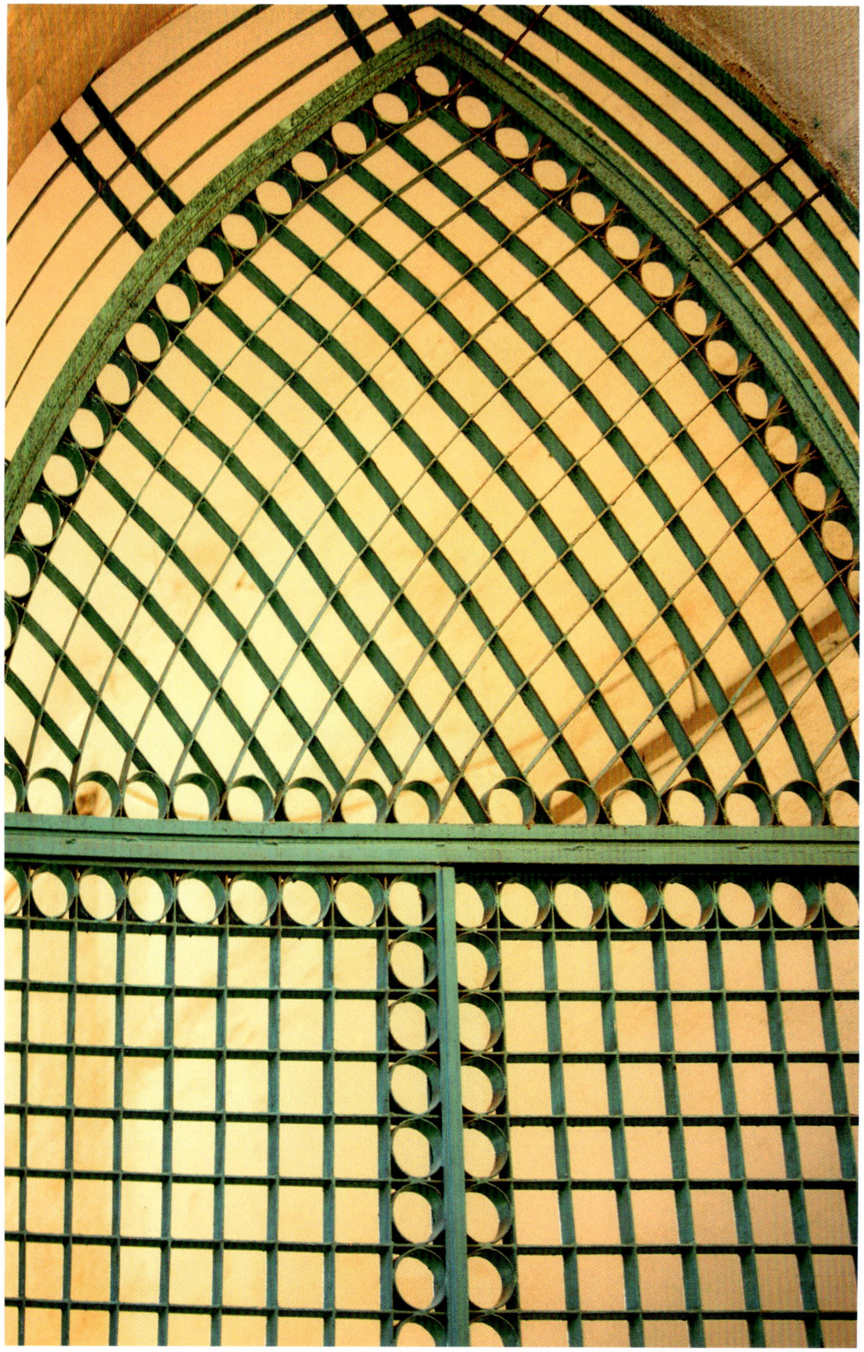

Intricate workmanship adorns many of the mosques that dot the countryside.

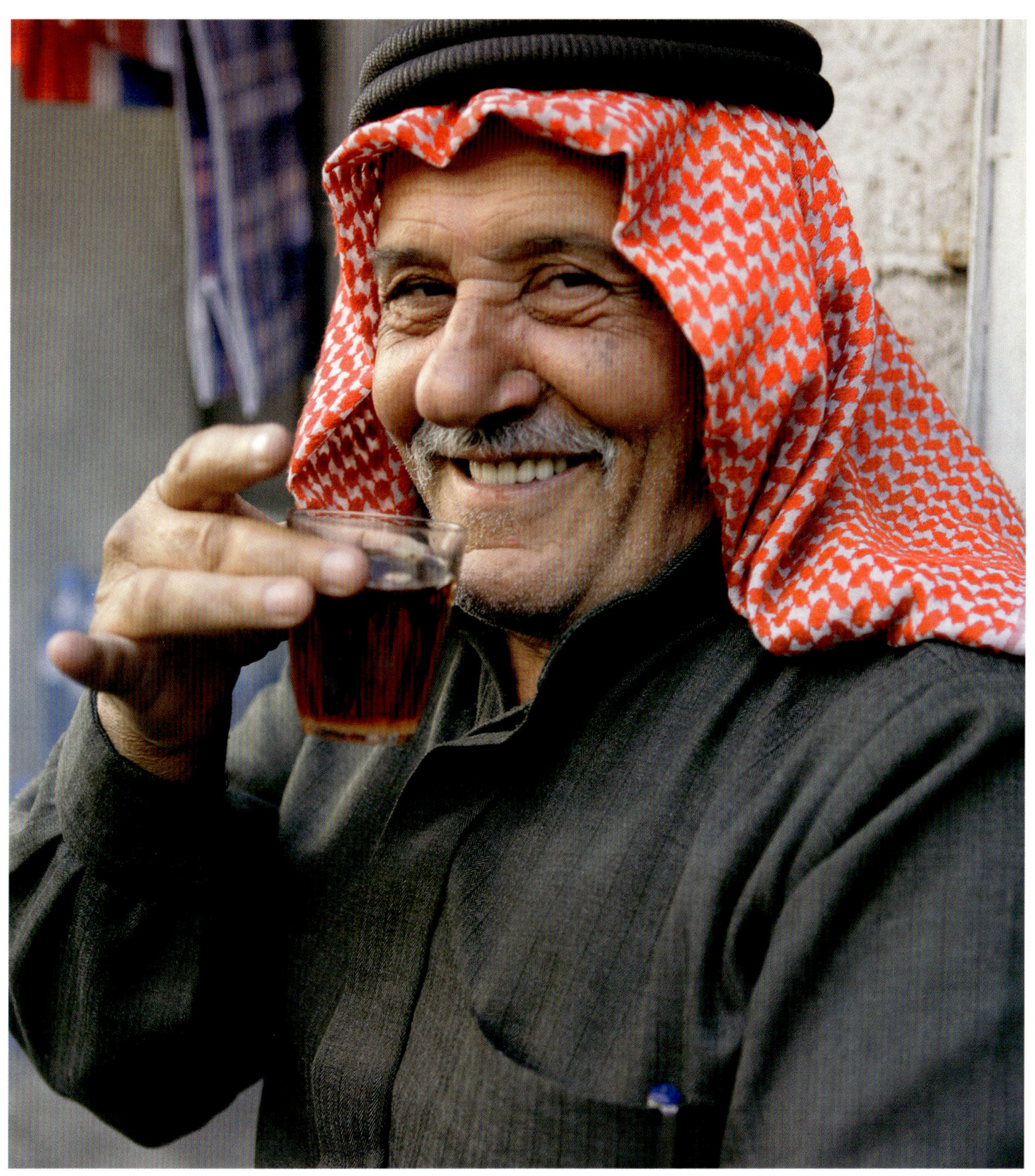

In coffee houses and street corners in Amman, men wearing traditional head scarves, or *kaffiyeh*, strike up conversations by offering a genuine smile, a deep voiced "Welcome", and a hot glass of Chai Tea.

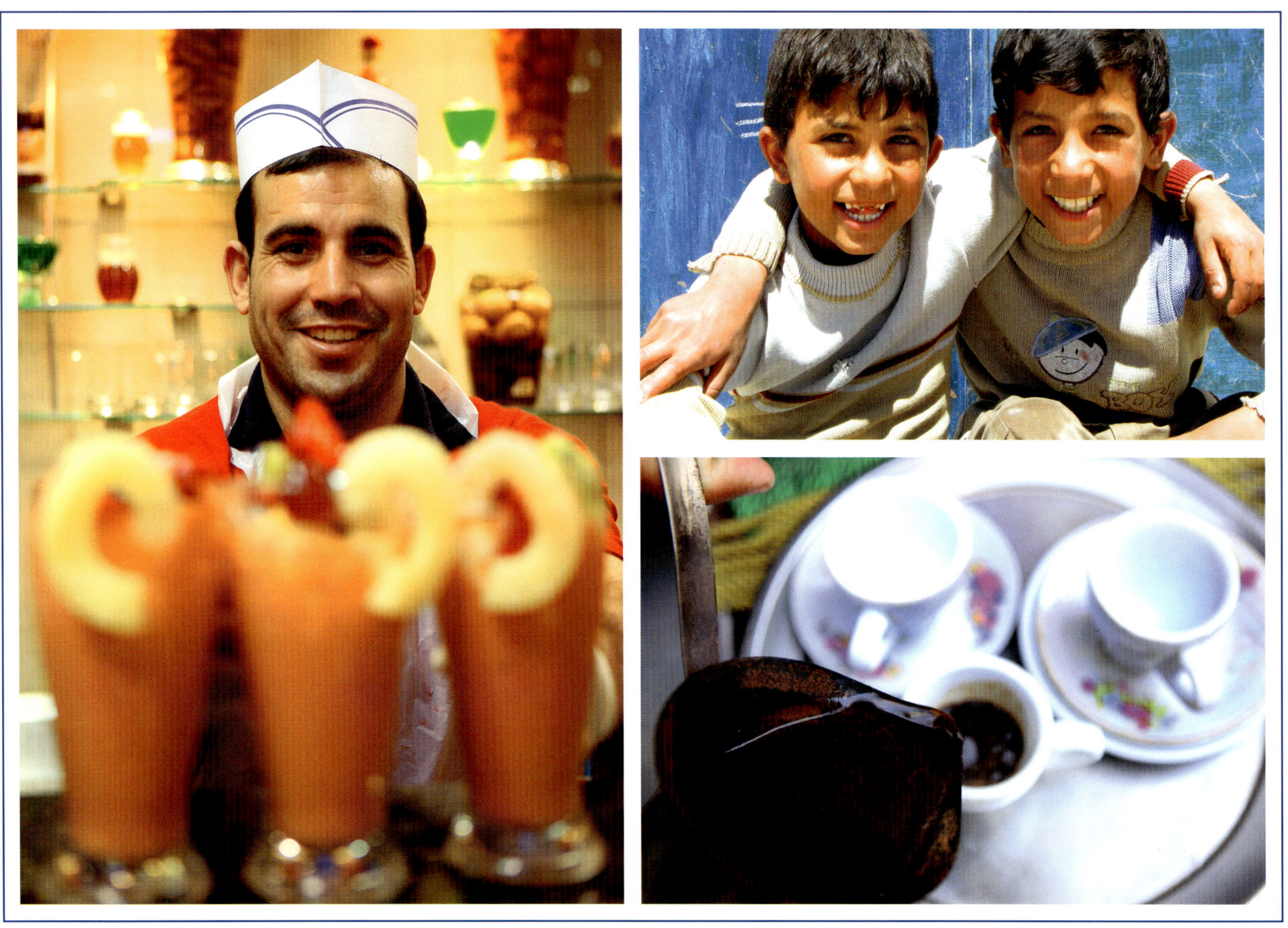

Warm and friendly faces greet you as you indulge in local fare and rejuvenate in the sun.

Jordan's window to the sea, Aqaba, is a modern beach resort where one can pass the days frolicking in the Red Sea.

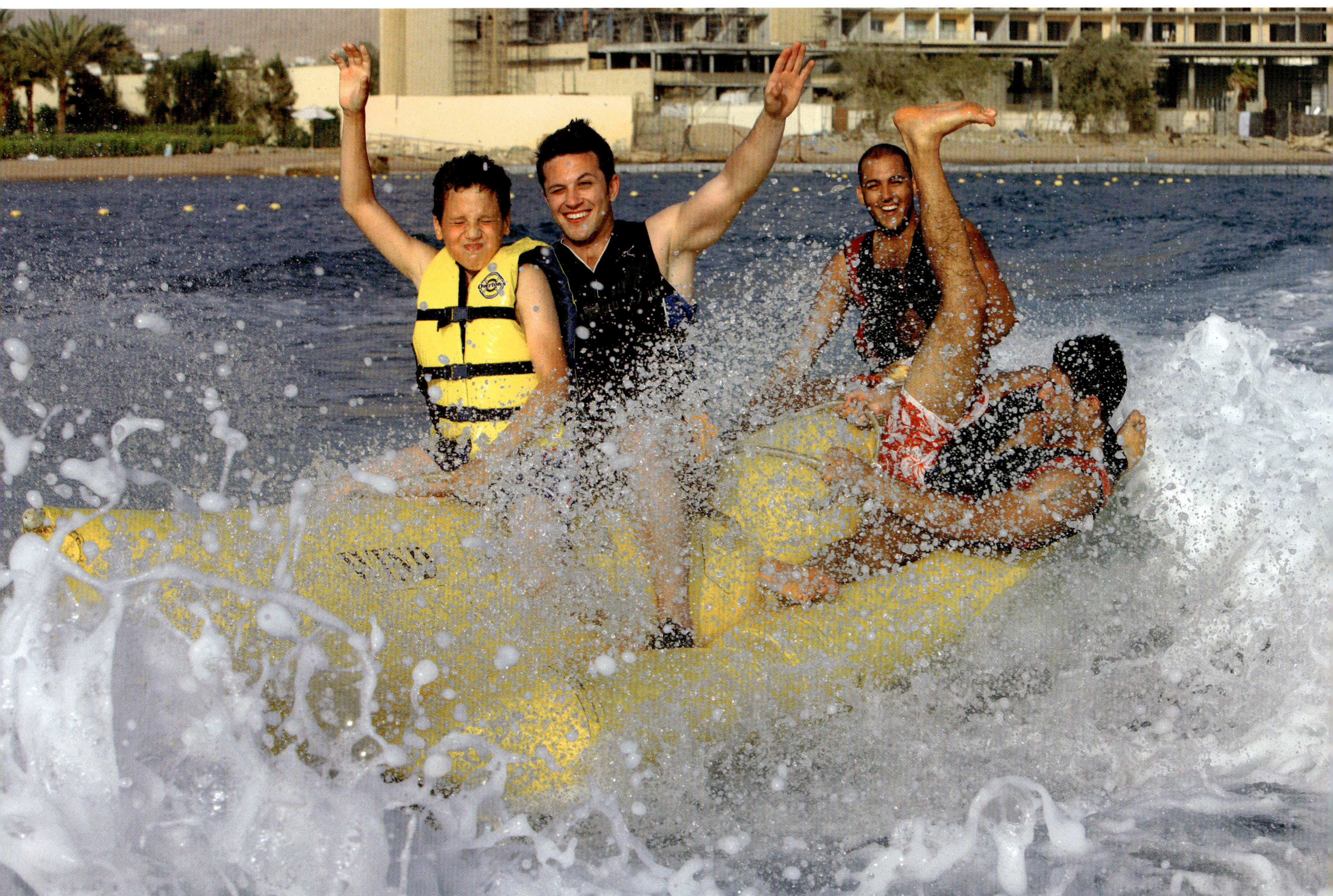

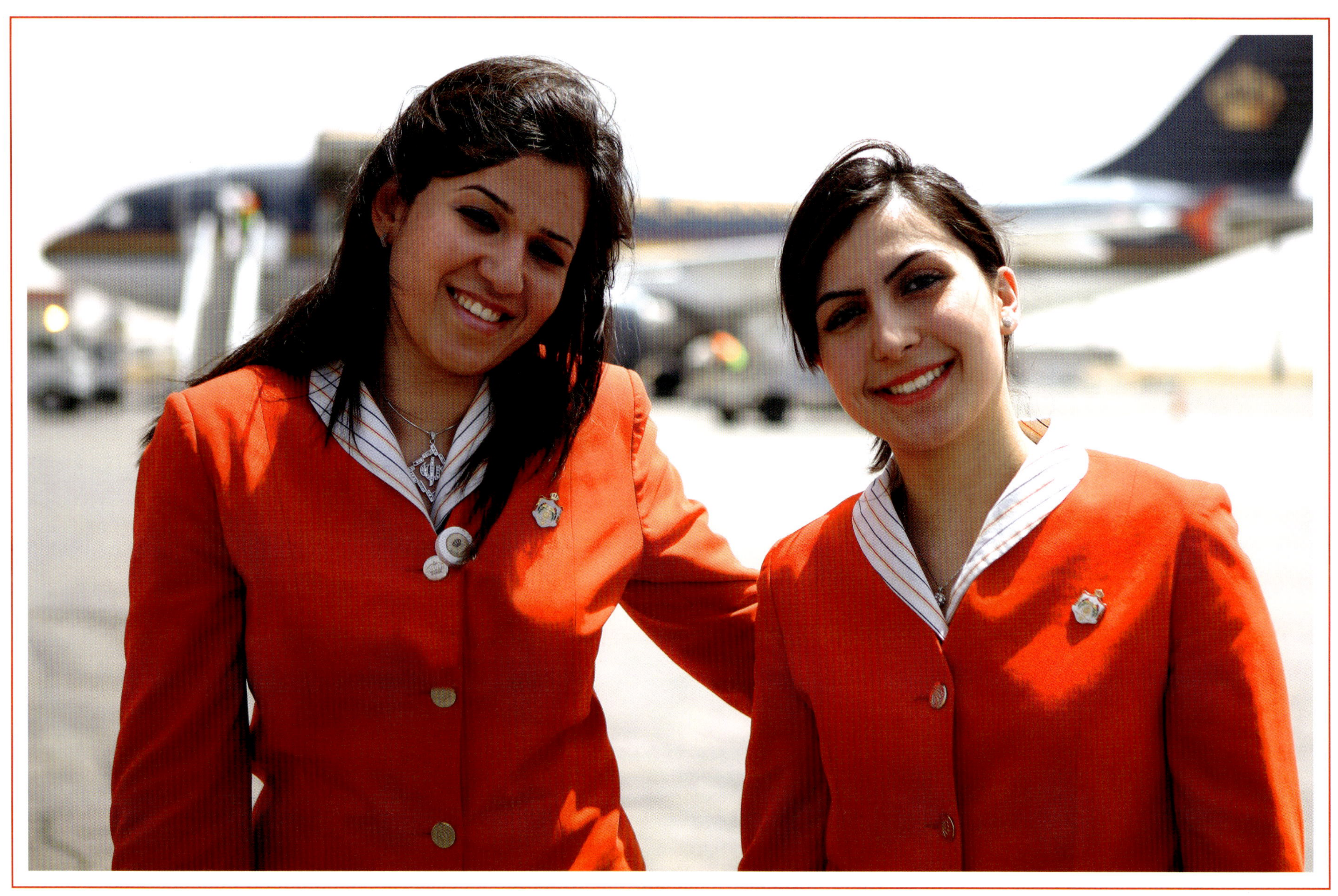

Flight attendants warmly greet passengers at Queen Alia International Airport – Jordan's gateway to the world.

Nestled between the Red Sea and the Sinai mountains, the beautiful port city of Aqaba twinkles in the early evening light.

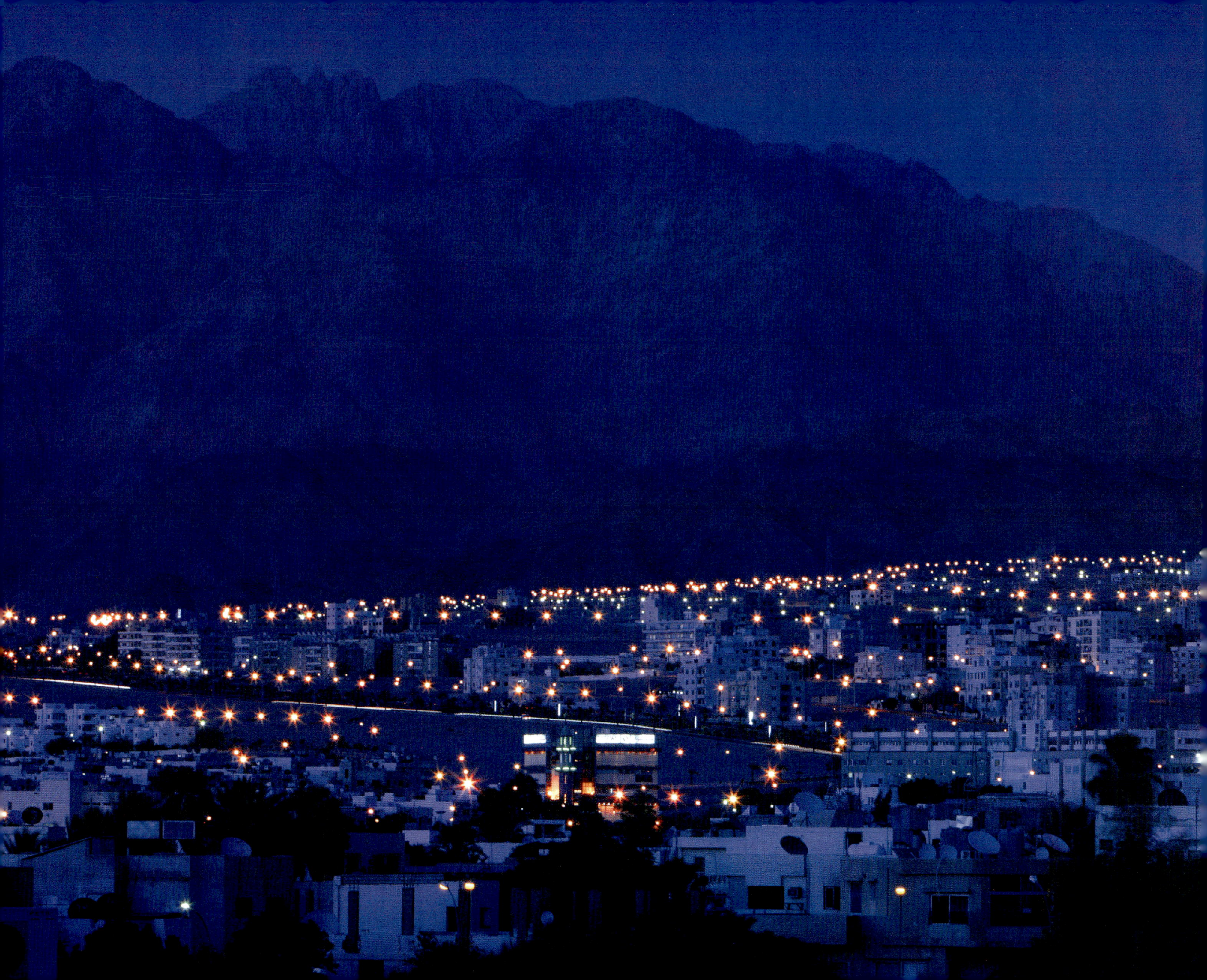

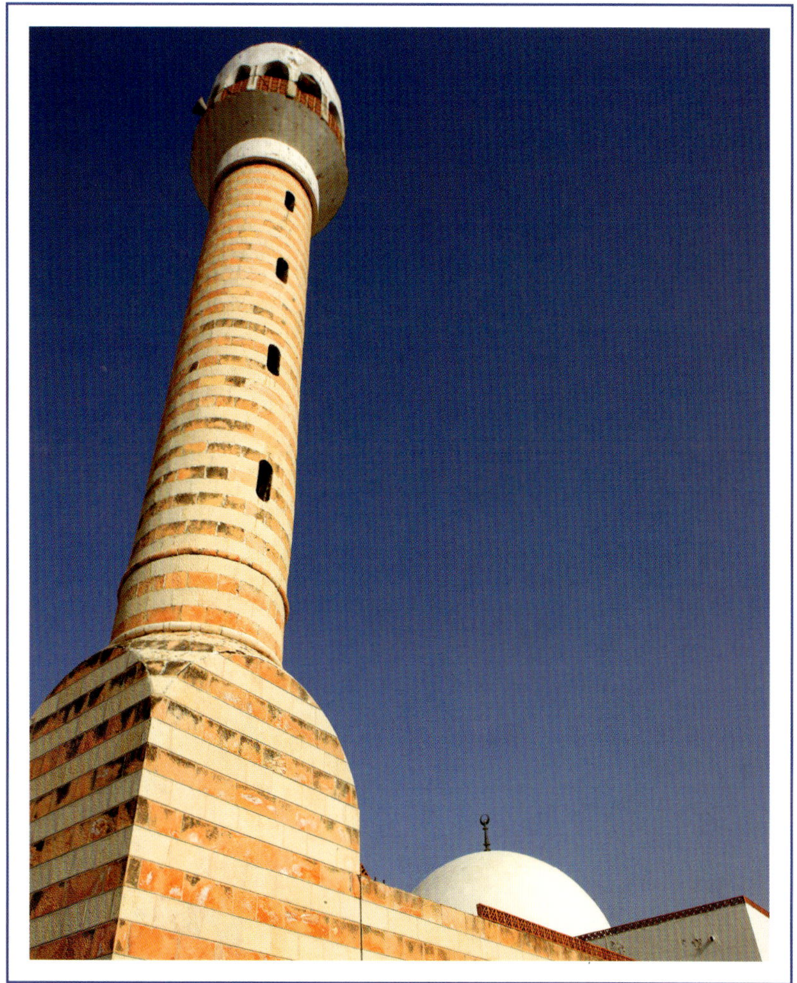

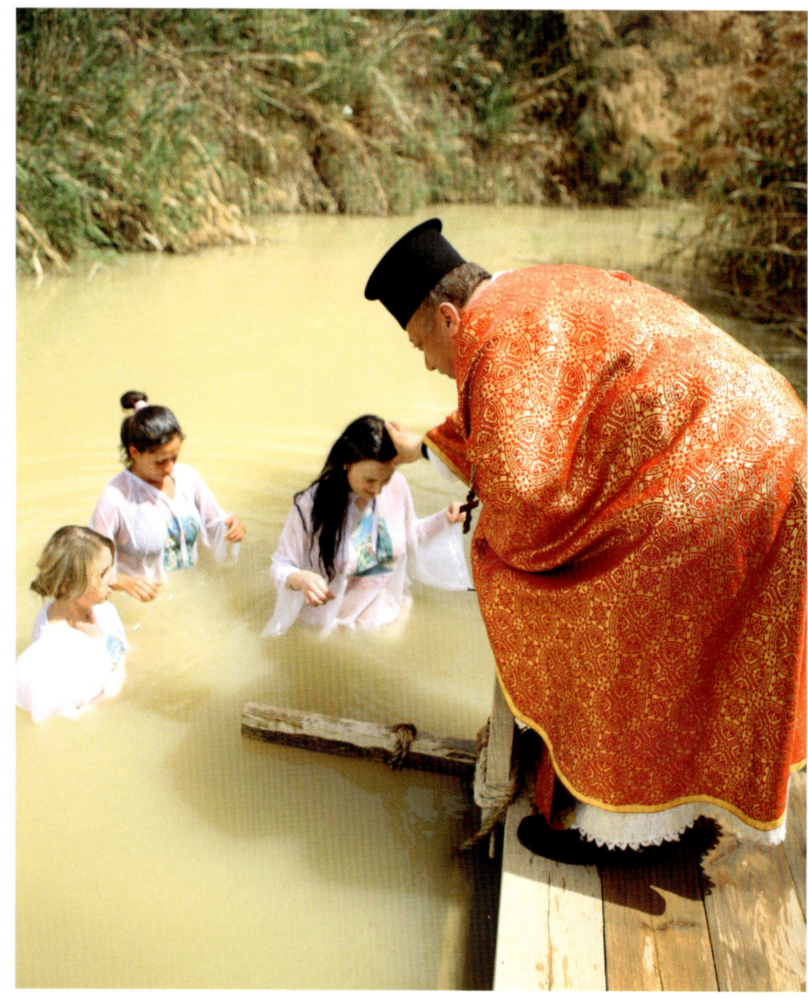

Crowning the highest point in As-Salt, sits the massive Jabal al-Qal'ah mosque whose haunting call to prayer resonates throughout the village far below.

Being baptized in the holy waters of the Jordan River by a Roman Catholic priest will forever be a cherished memory for these three young girls from Poland.

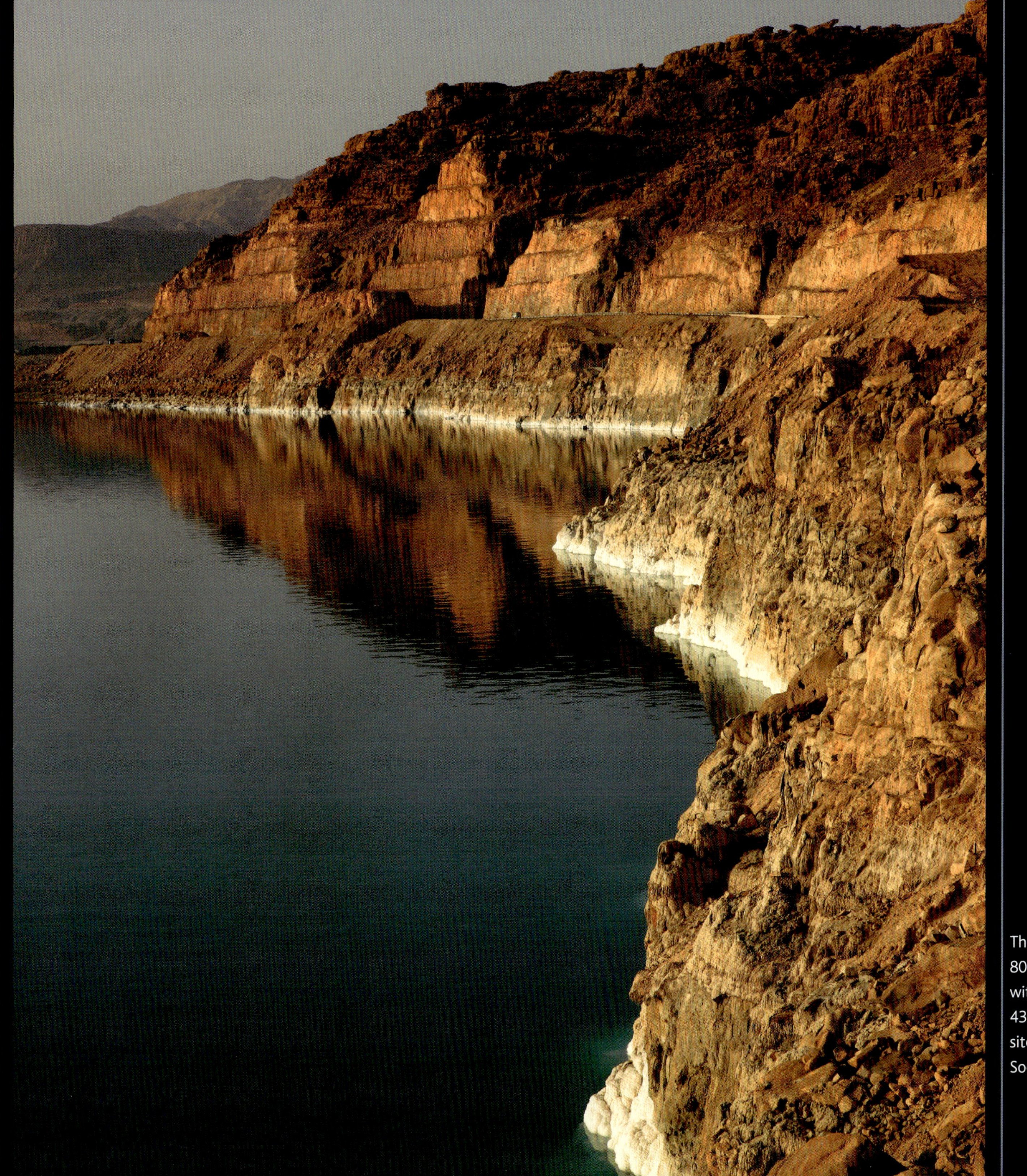

The Dead Sea, approximately 80 km long and 14 km wide with a maximum depth of 430 m, is believed to be the site of the ancient cities of Sodom and Gomorrah.

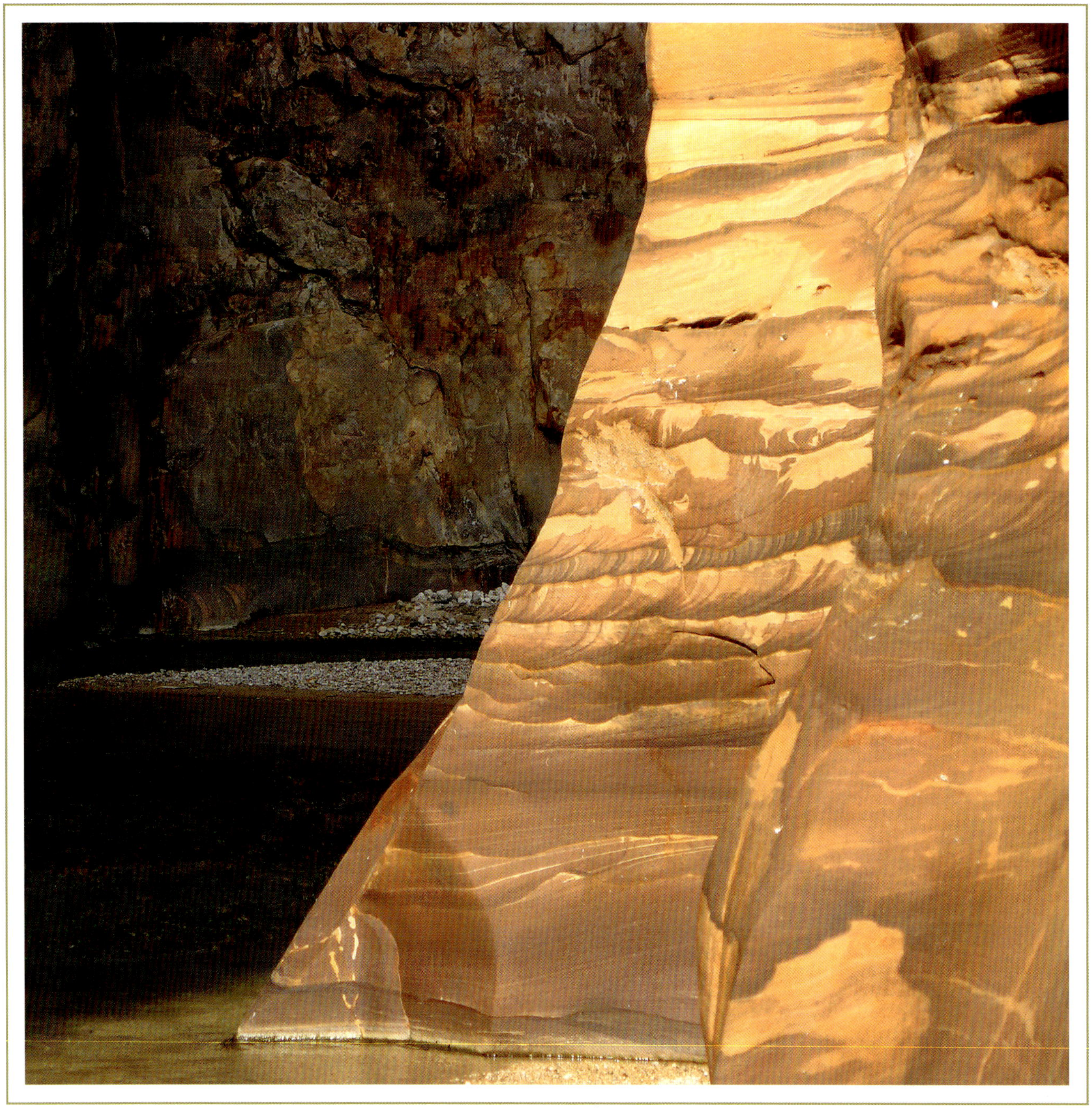

Striated sandstone cliffs provide a kaleidoscope of reflecting colors within the Wadi Mujib, sometimes referred to as the Grand Canyon of Jordan.

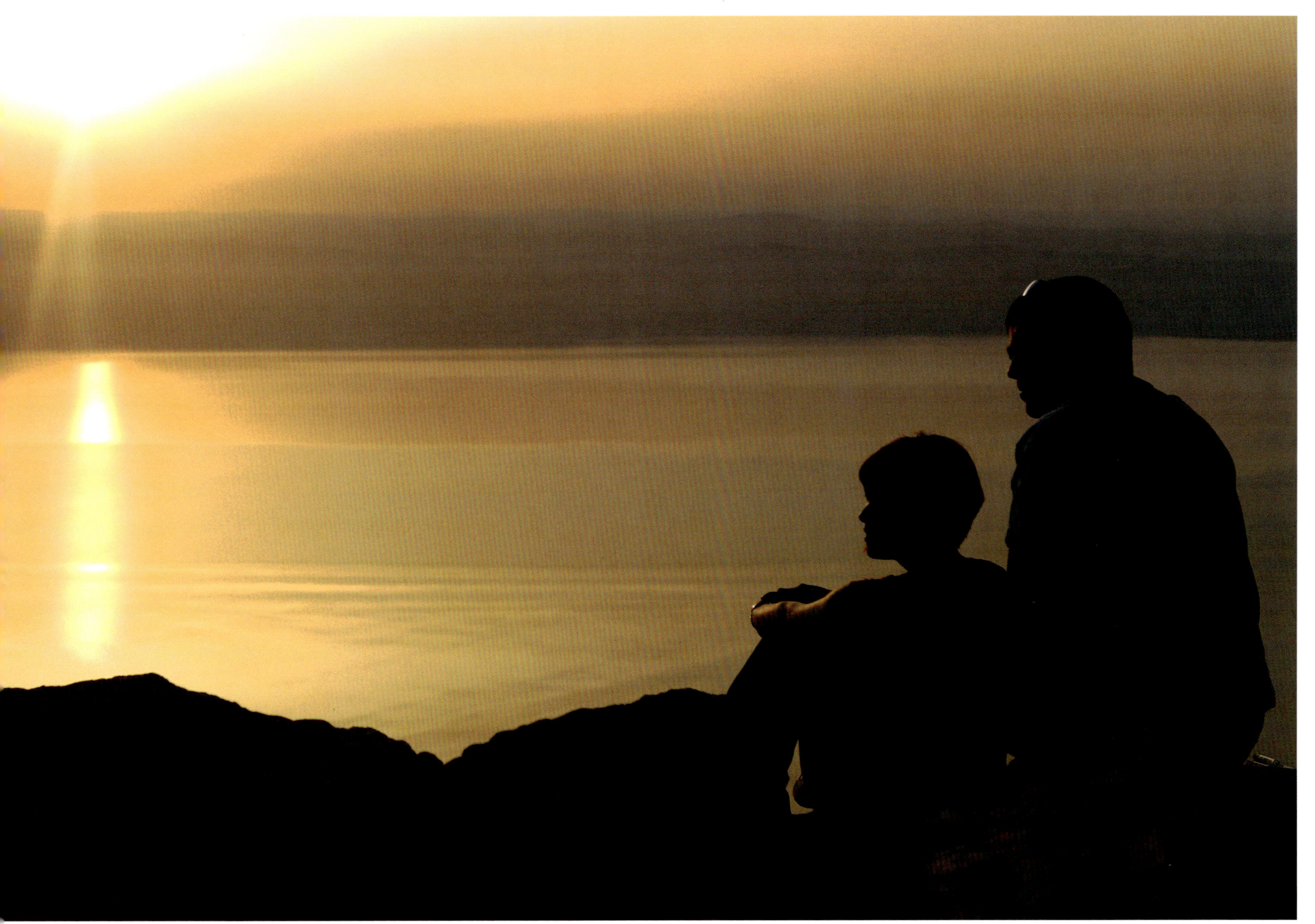

The Dead Sea Panoramic Complex is the perfect spot to savor a majestic sunset over the Dead Sea.

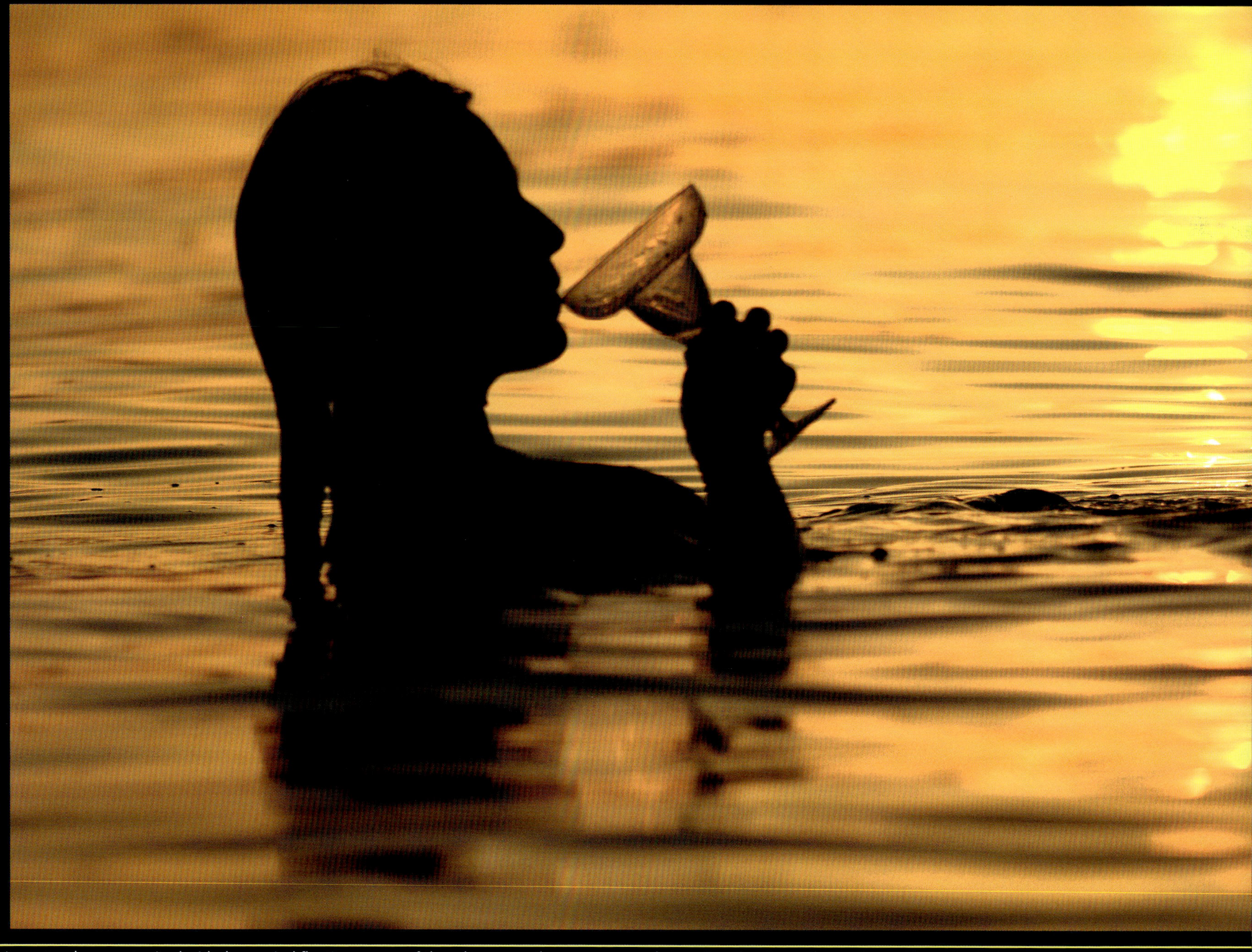

A spectacular sunset mixed with the magical floating powers of the salty sea soothes away care and stress. Travelers from all over the world, and Jordanians wanting a getaway, come to be pampered at one of the many resort hotels, including the luxurious Movenpick Dead Sea Spa which offers the healing powers of the sea's minerals and mud.

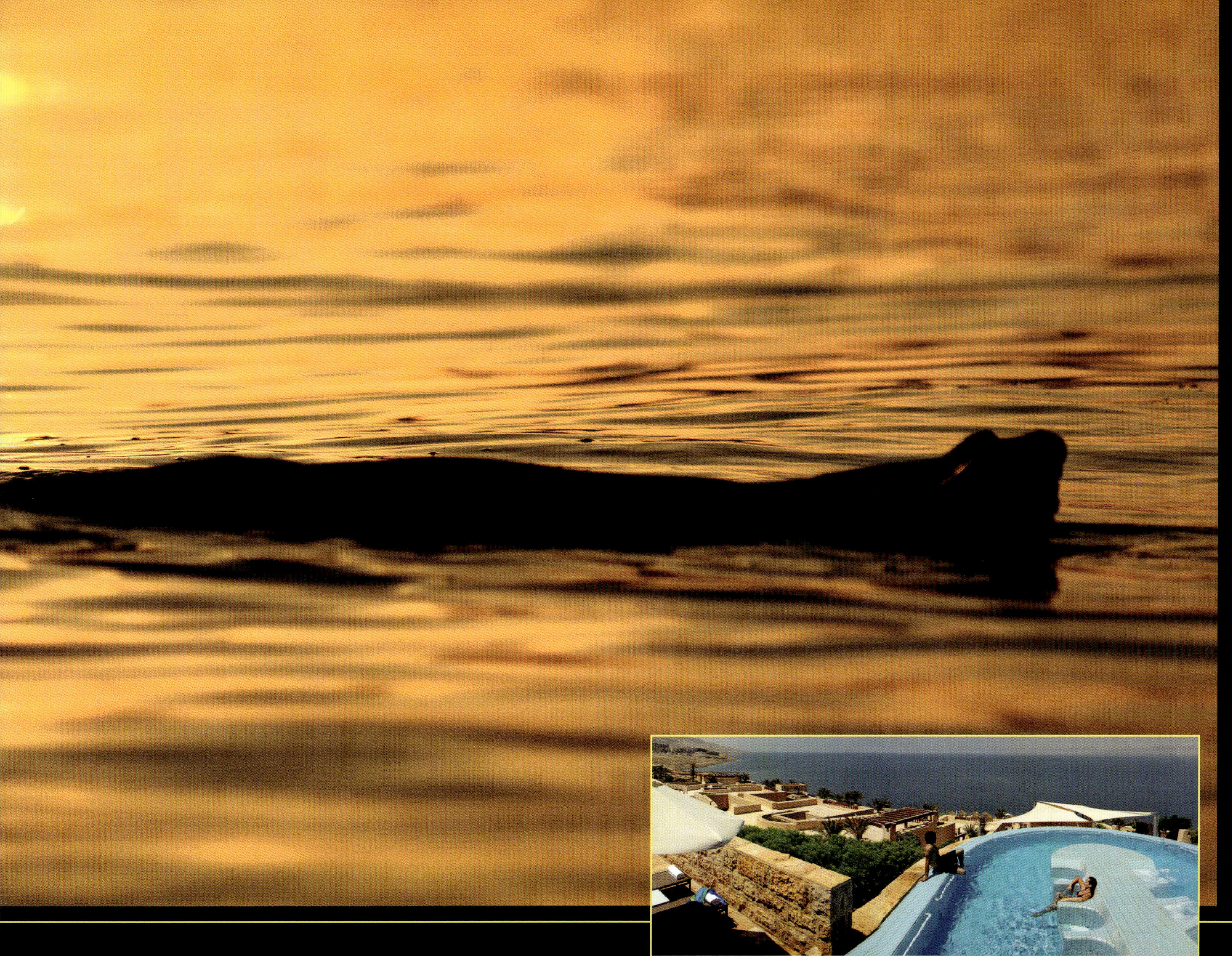

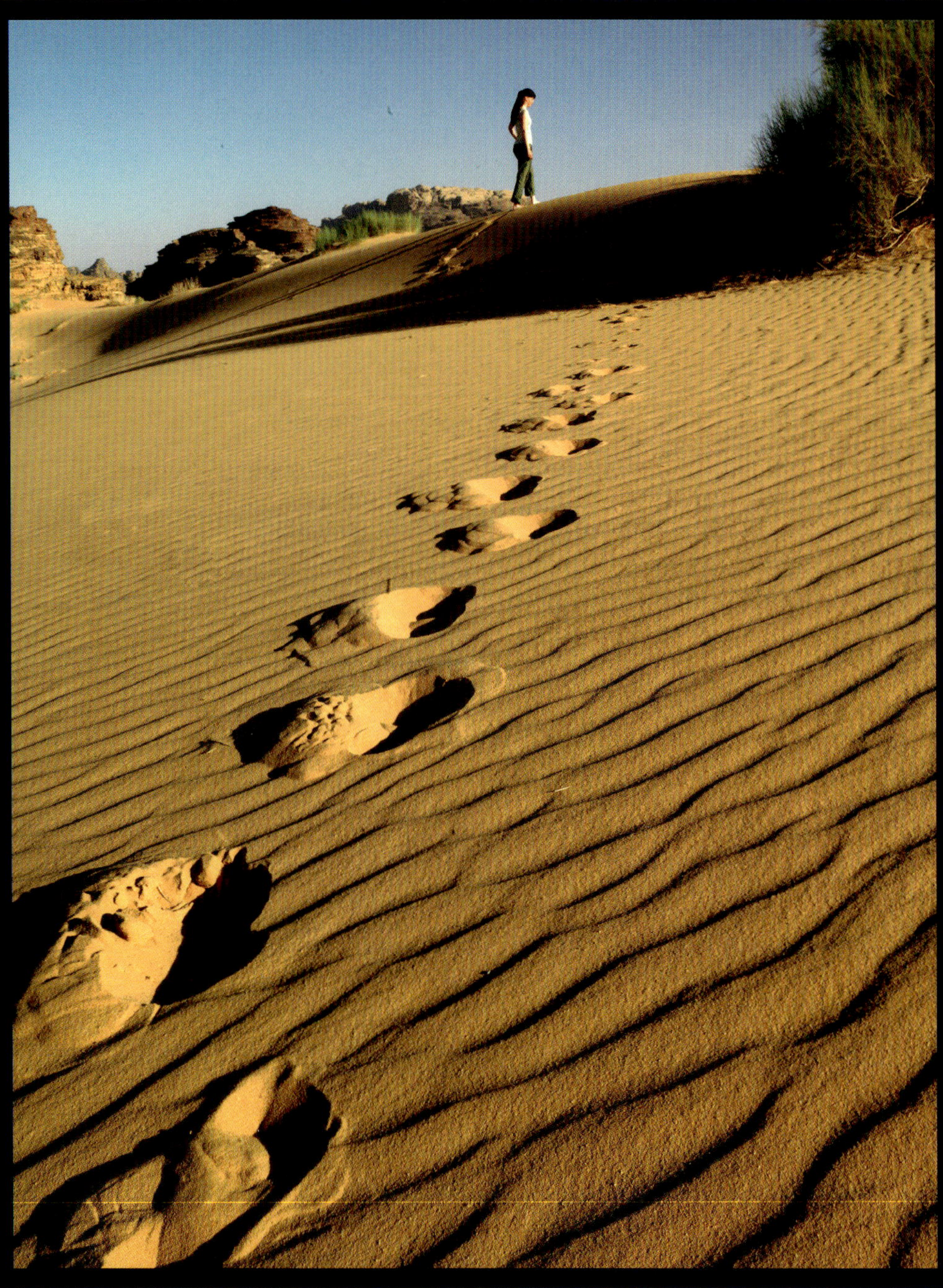

The restored Roman Theatre in Amman, with a capacity of 6,000 spectators is still in use year-round. Dating back to the 2nd century A.D., these lofty heights accommodated the ordinary citizens who would look down on the noblemen, seated near the stage.

The shifting sands of time in the Wadi Rum bear witness to a timeless place, virtually untouched by humans.

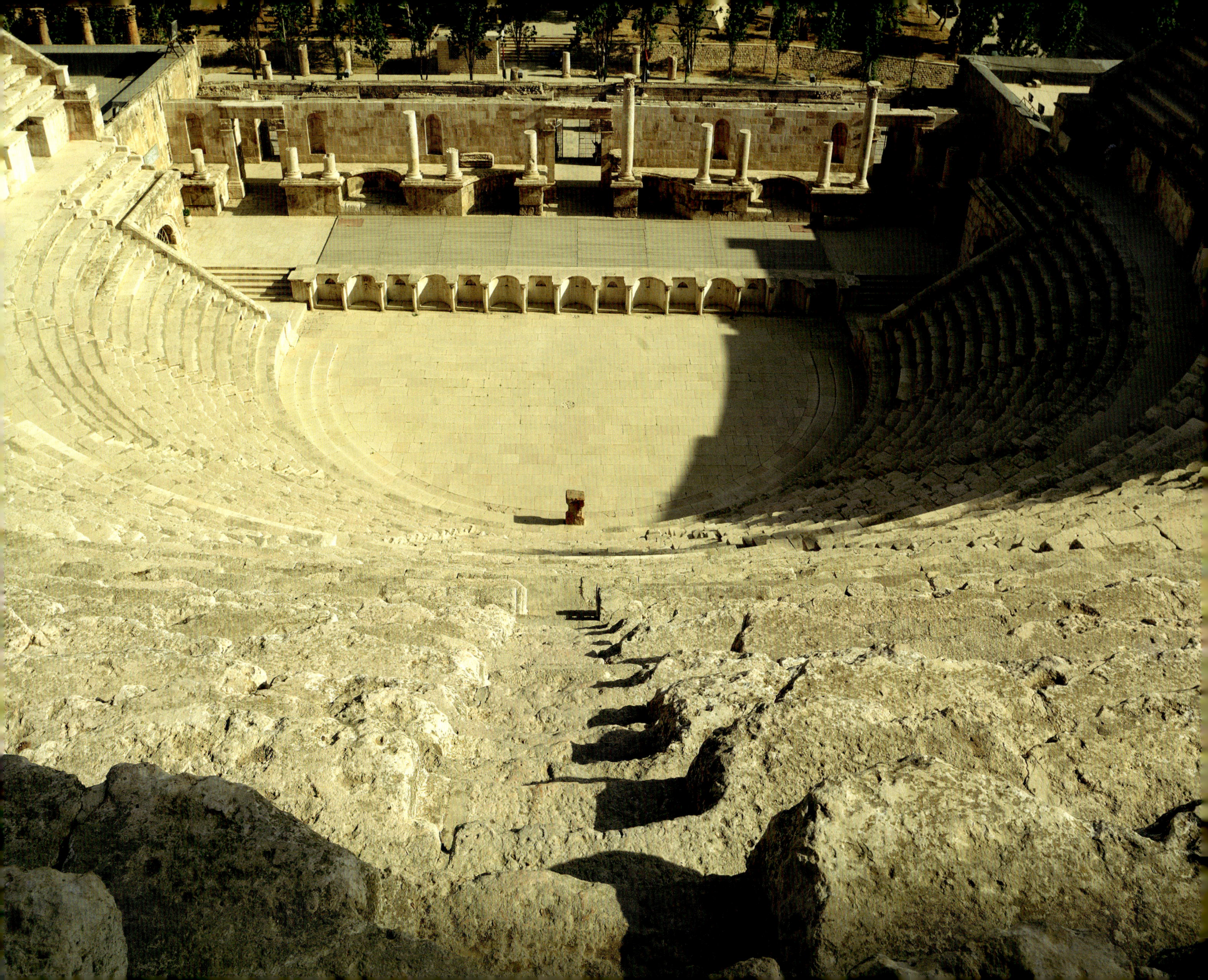

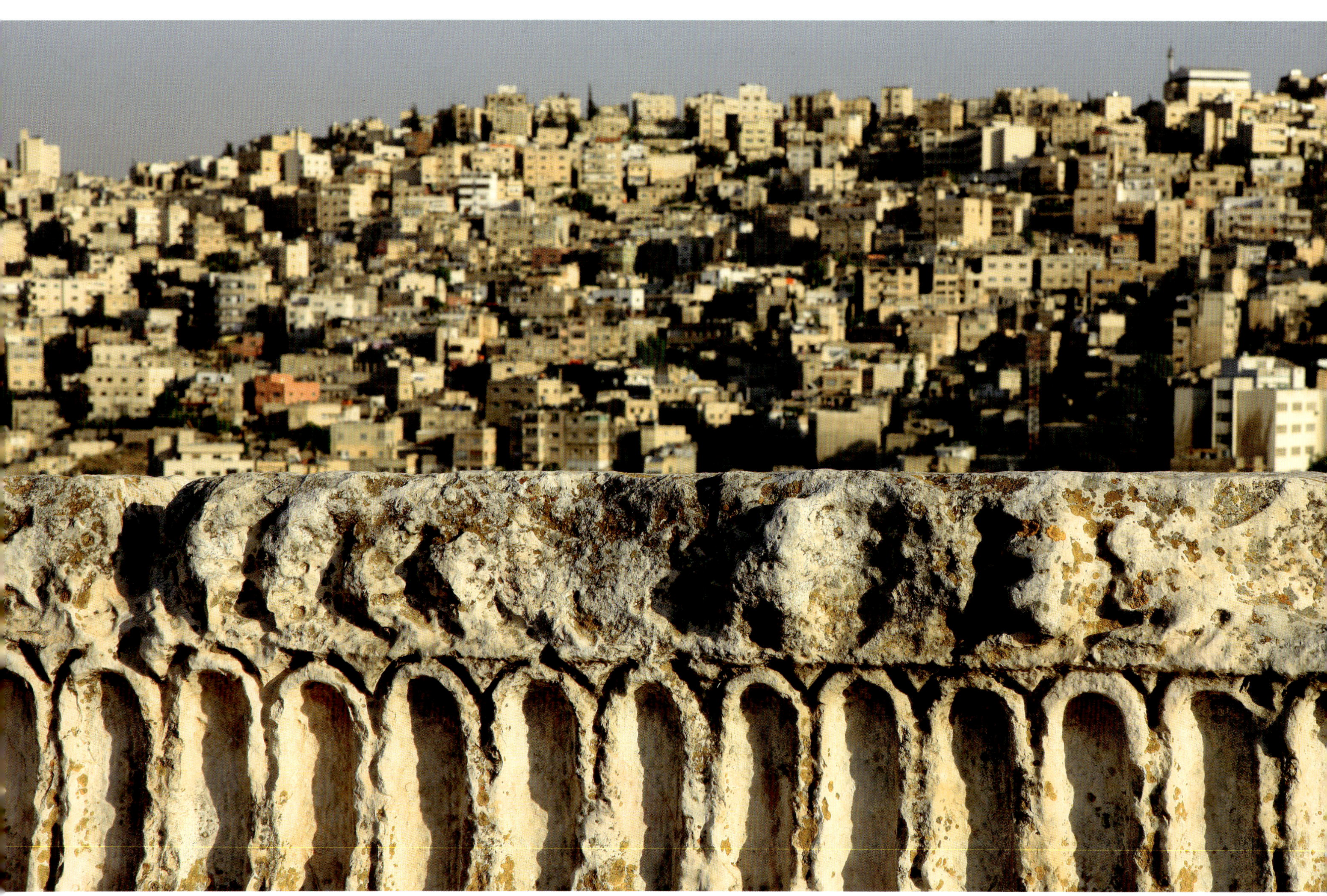

Amman, the capital of Jordan, is a fascinating city of contrasts where new and old blend seamlessly, as seen here on Citadel Hill.

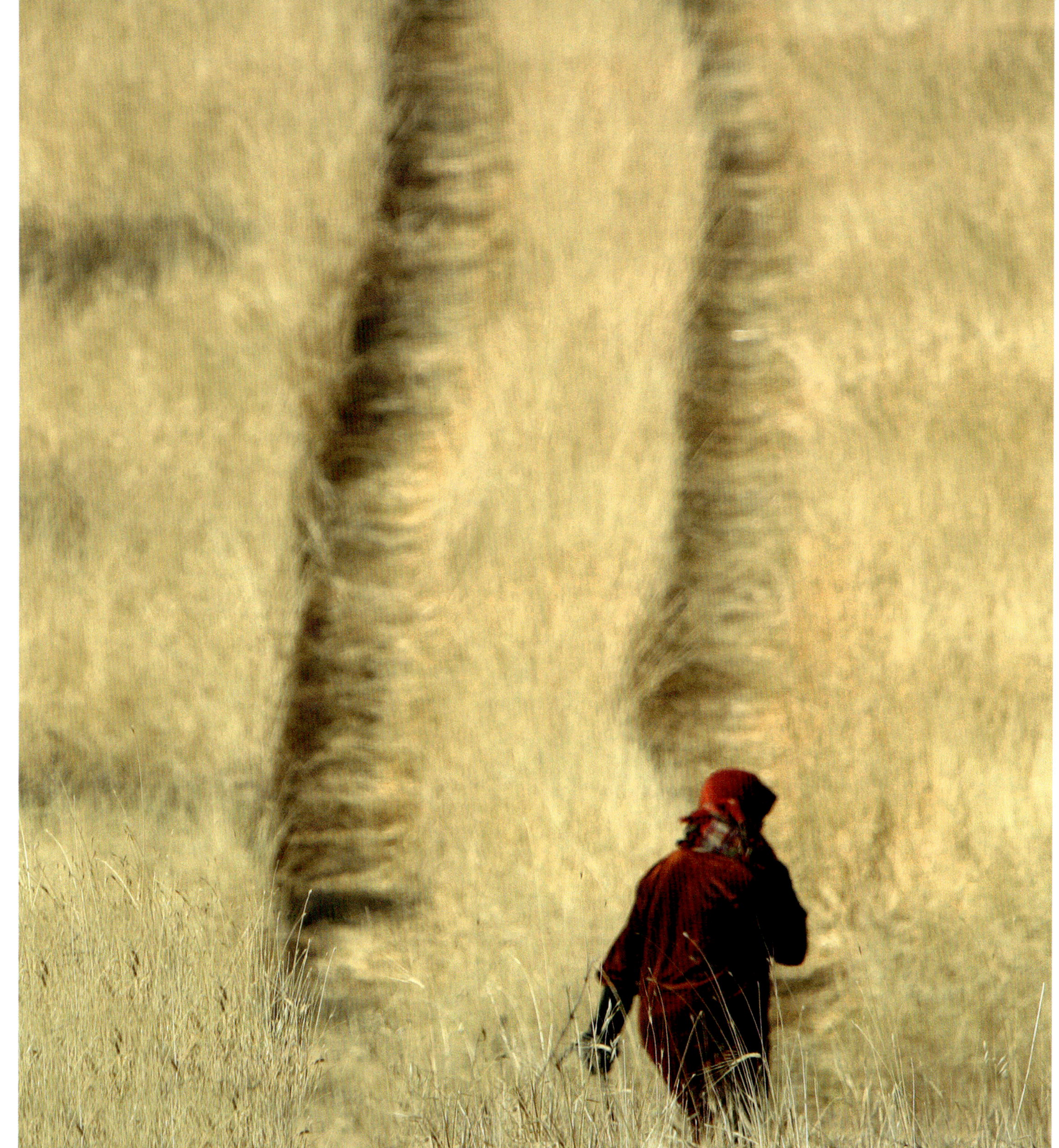

A Bedouin woman in brightly colored traditional clothing crosses a golden field to tend to her grazing flock of sheep. The word Bedouin is derived from Bedu, meaning "nomadic".

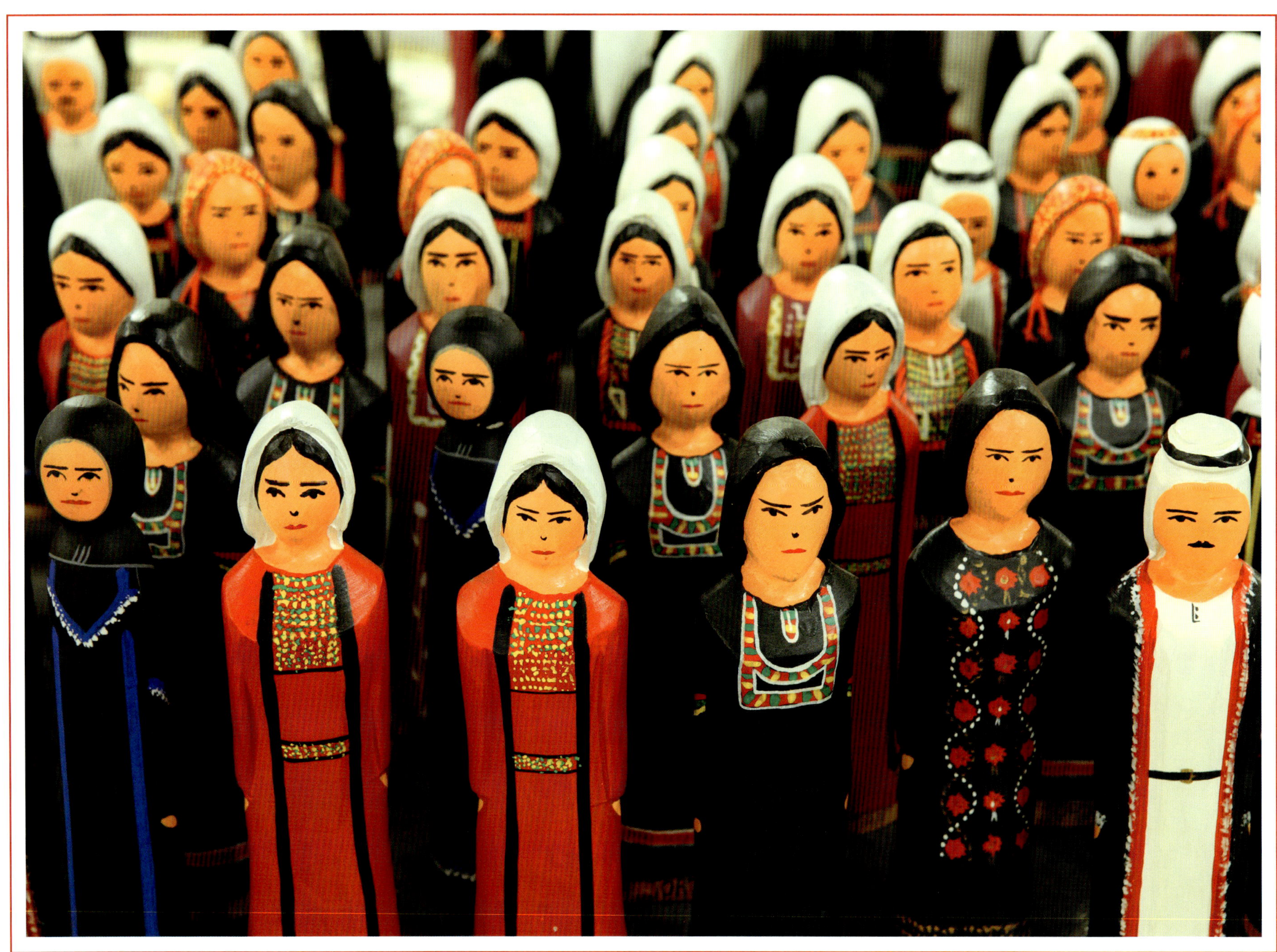

Miniature wooden dolls stand at attention at a souvenir store in Madaba waiting to be plucked off the shelf. The colorful gifts portray men and women in costumes representative of regions associated with a specific tribe or village.

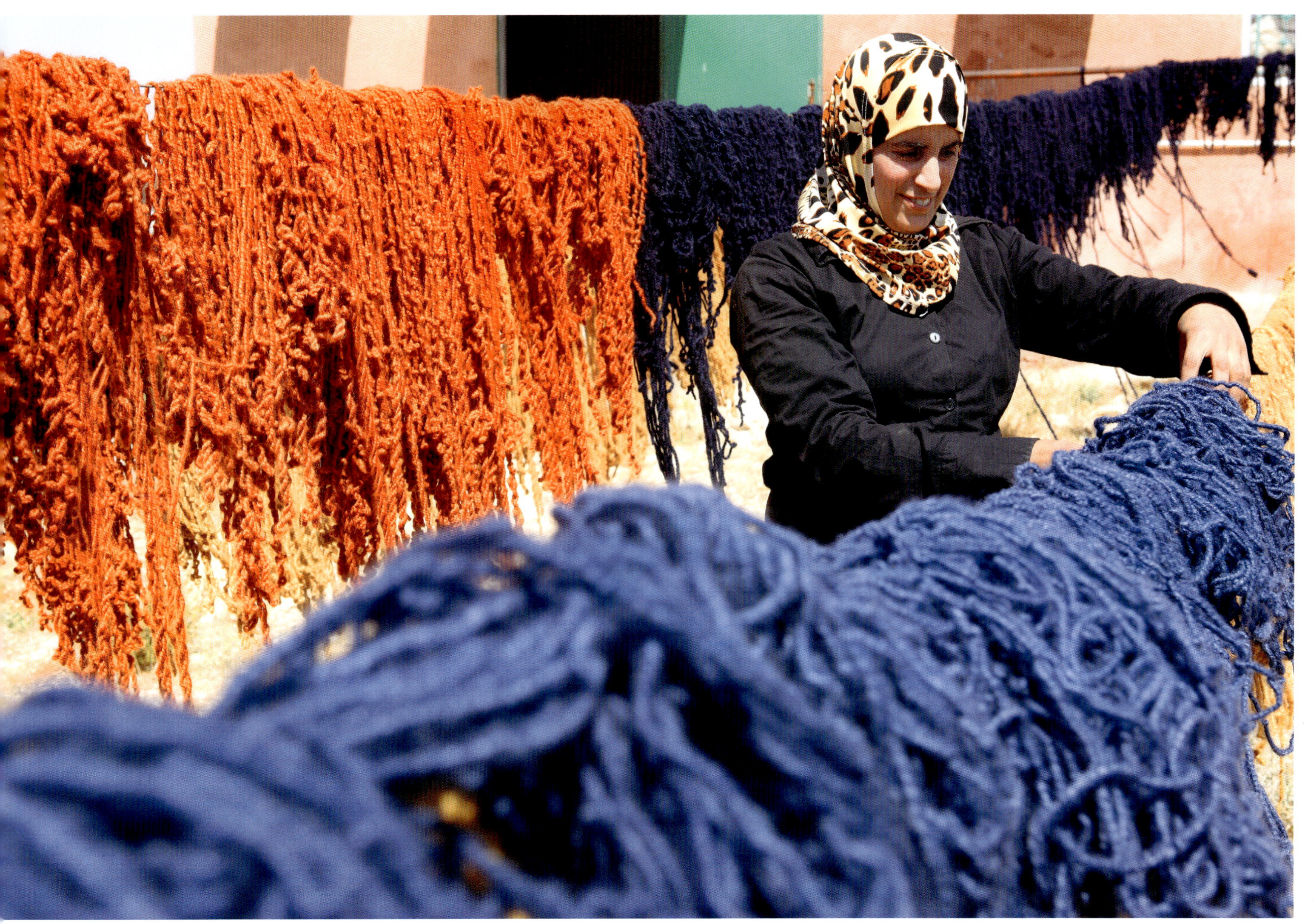

Freshly dyed wool is hung to drip dry in the warm sunshine. The Bani Hamida Women's Weaving Project near Mukawir produces some of the finest wool rugs in all of Jordan.

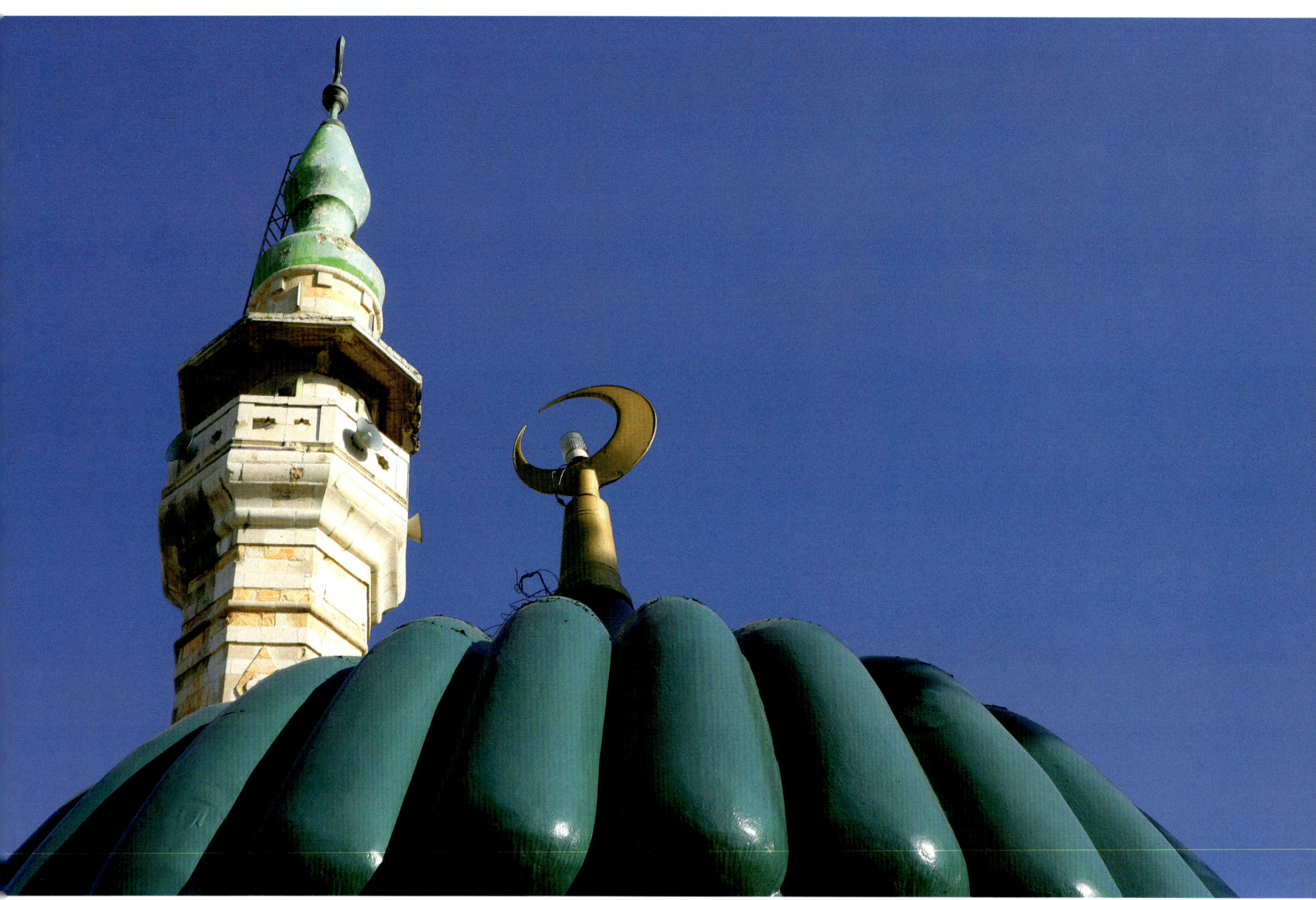

An ornate and colorful dome on a mosque in Amman.

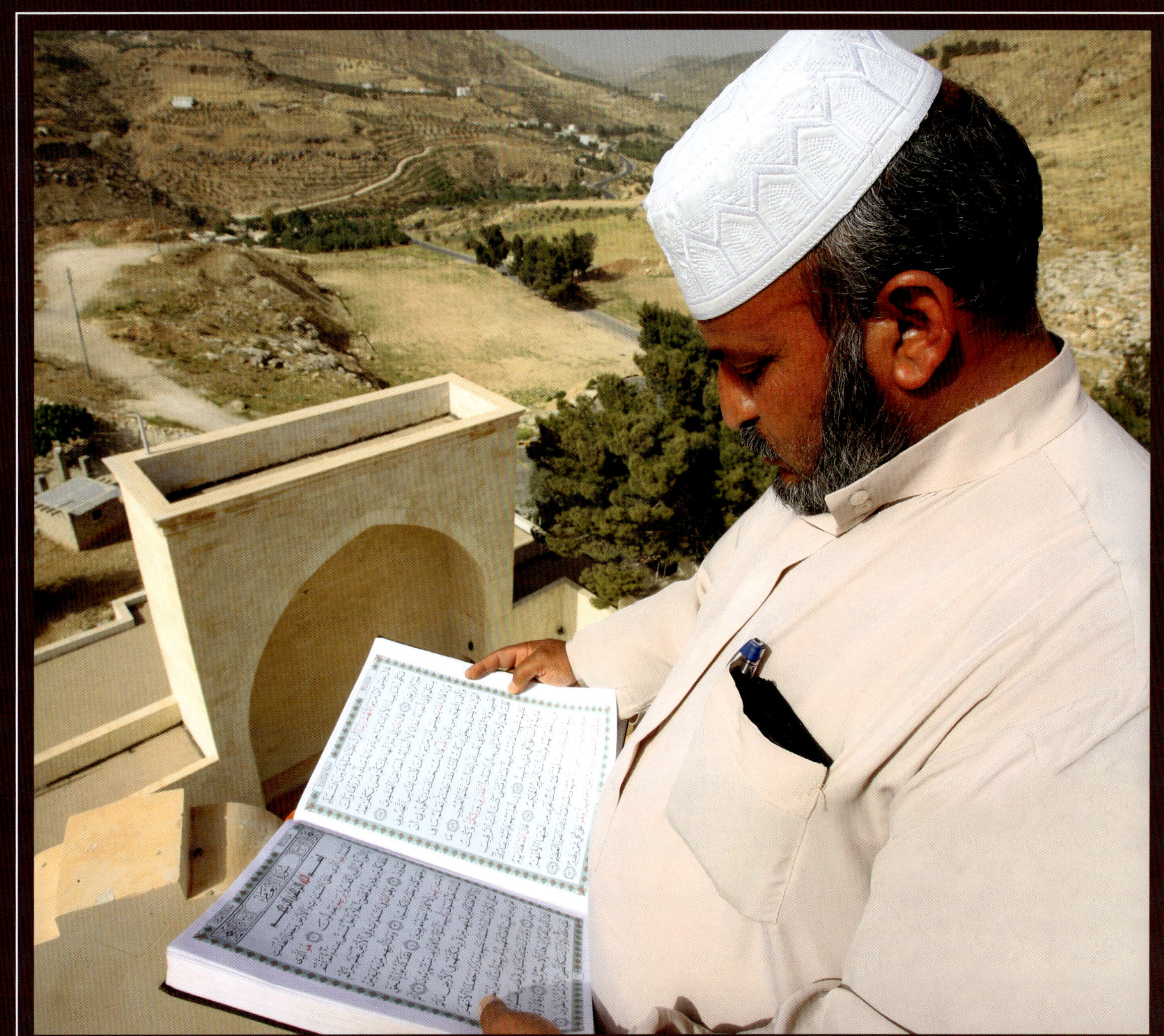

In a mosque high above the fertile hills around As-Salt, a Sheikh reads the Holy Qur'an of Islam.

A hiker peers out from behind a massive boulder at the Dana Nature Reserve. Composed of a chain of valleys and mountains stretching across the Jordan Rift Valley, the reserve is managed by the Royal Society for the Conservation of Nature.

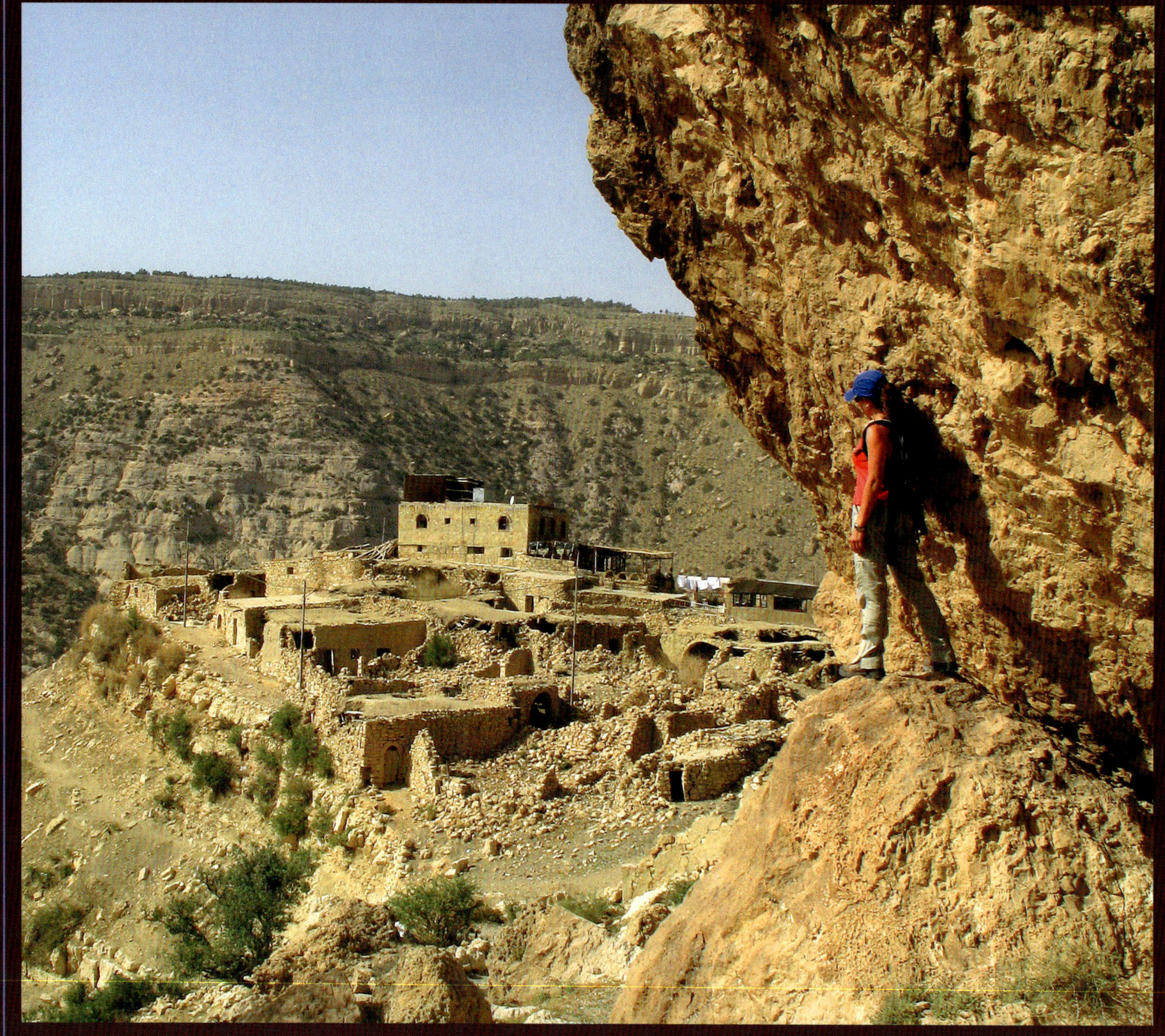

A fine example of the many different Minaret styles of architecture throughout Jordan.

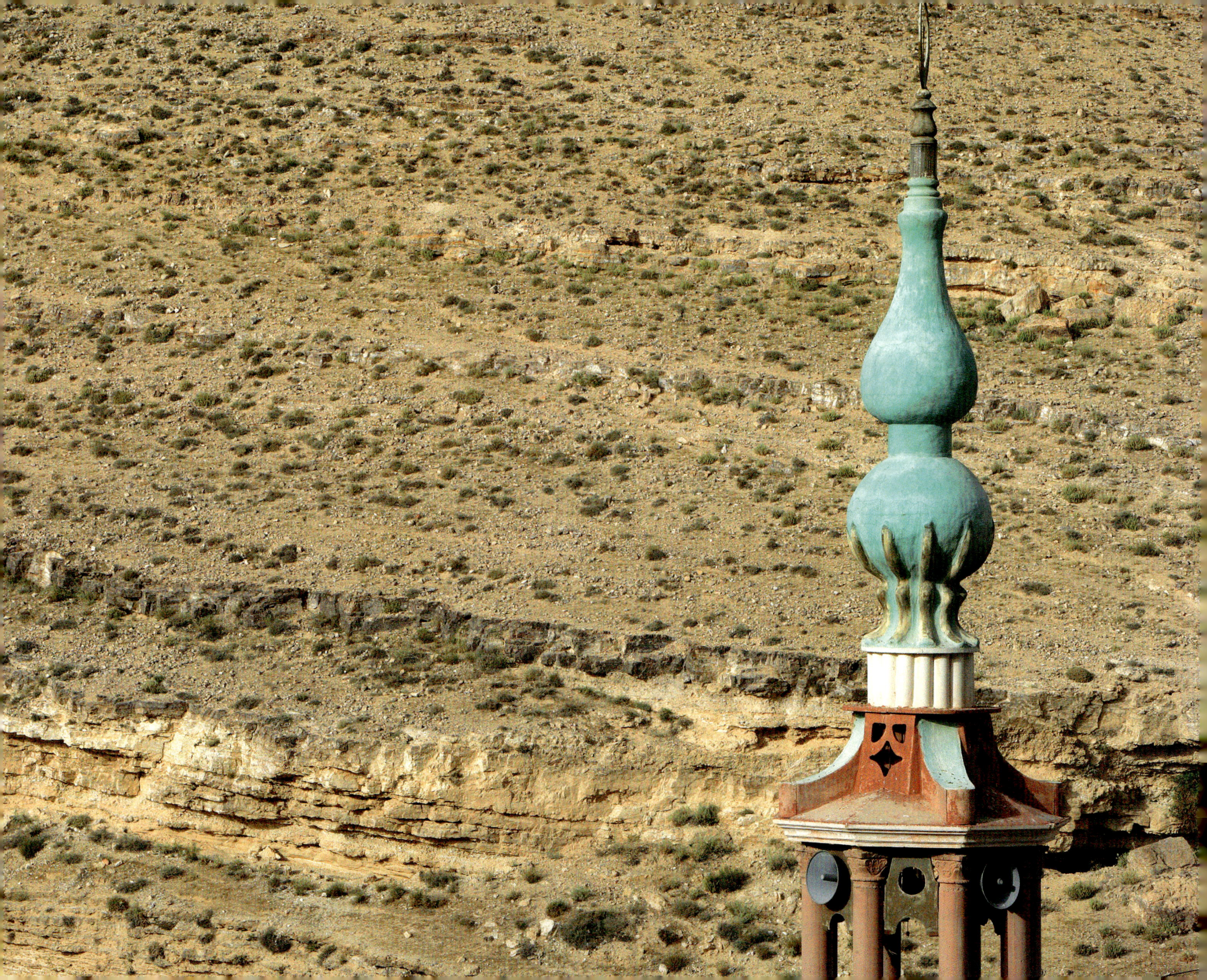

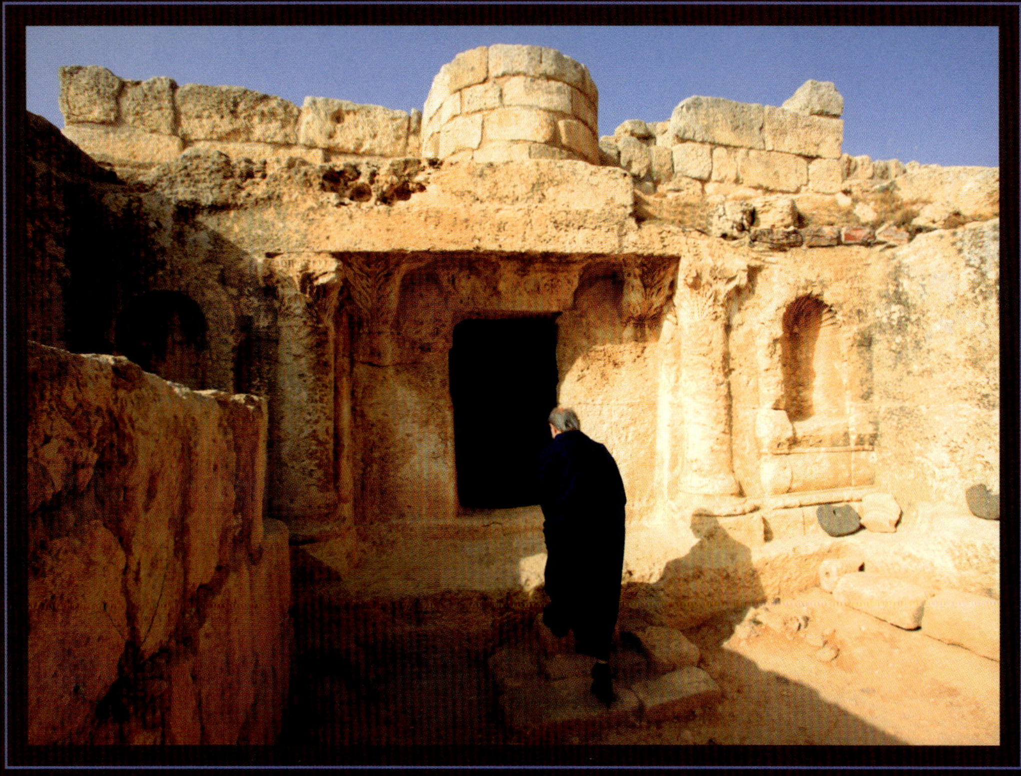

A devout clergyman enters the Cave of the Seven Sleepers or *Ahl, al-Kahf*. Located in a southern suburb of Amman, the cave contains seven sarcophagi. Legend tells of seven young Christian men who hid in this cave to escape Roman religious persecution and God put them to sleep for hundreds of years.

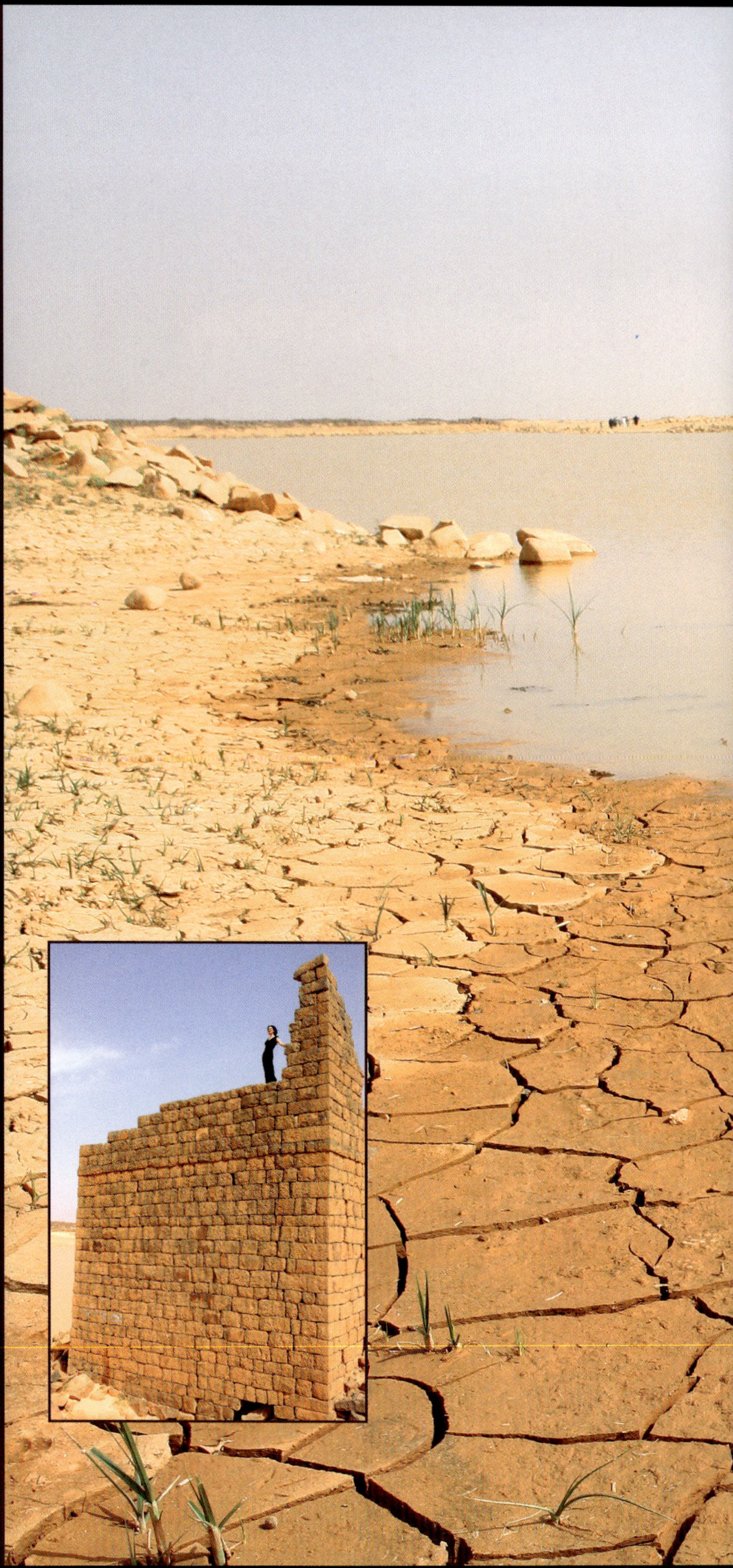

In the scorching eastern desert known as the Badia lies one of Jordan's most remote attractions. The crumbling castle, Burqu, is a mirage-like apparition that appears to float on the shores of Ghadir Burqu – a 2 km long lake that bakes in the desert sun.

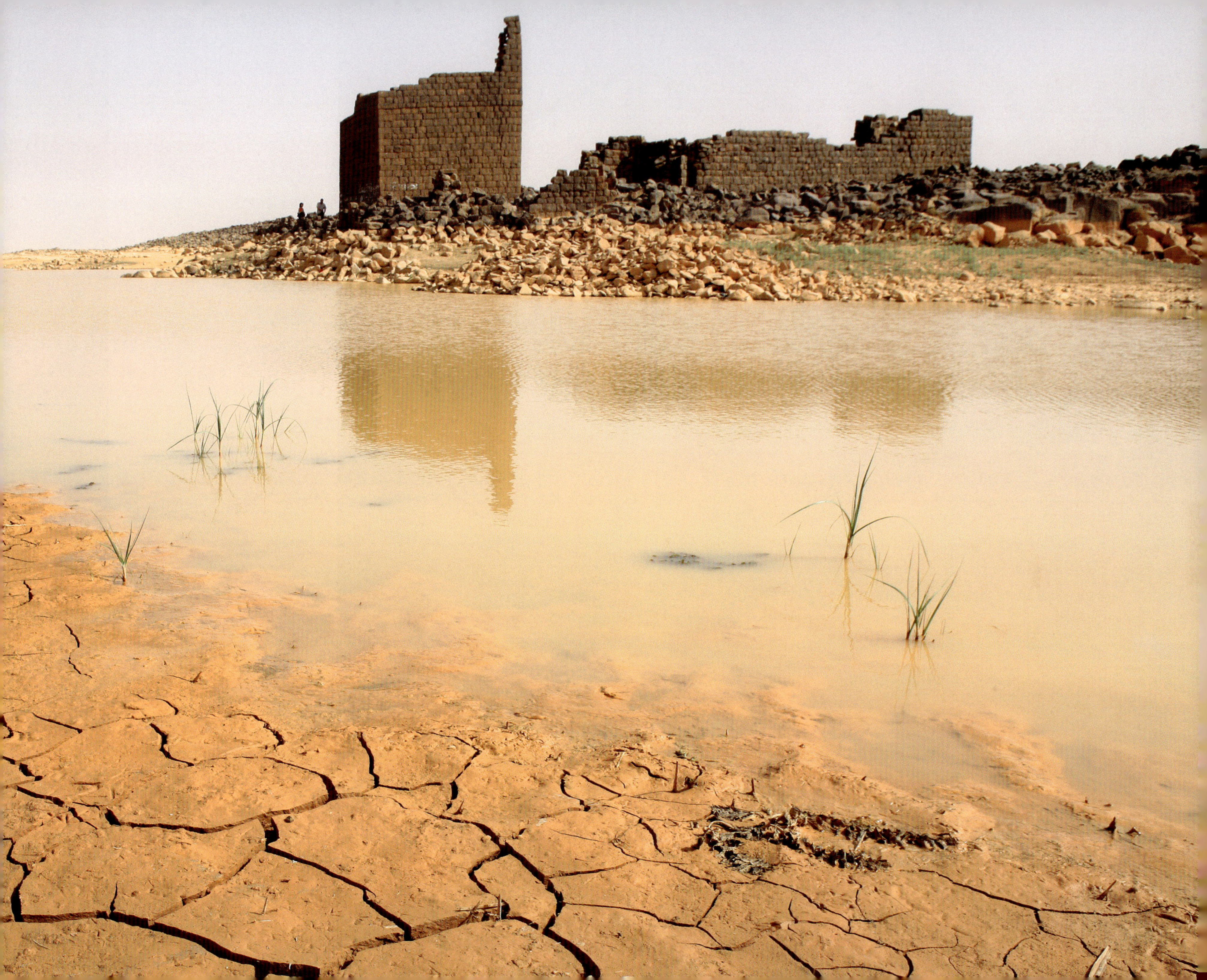

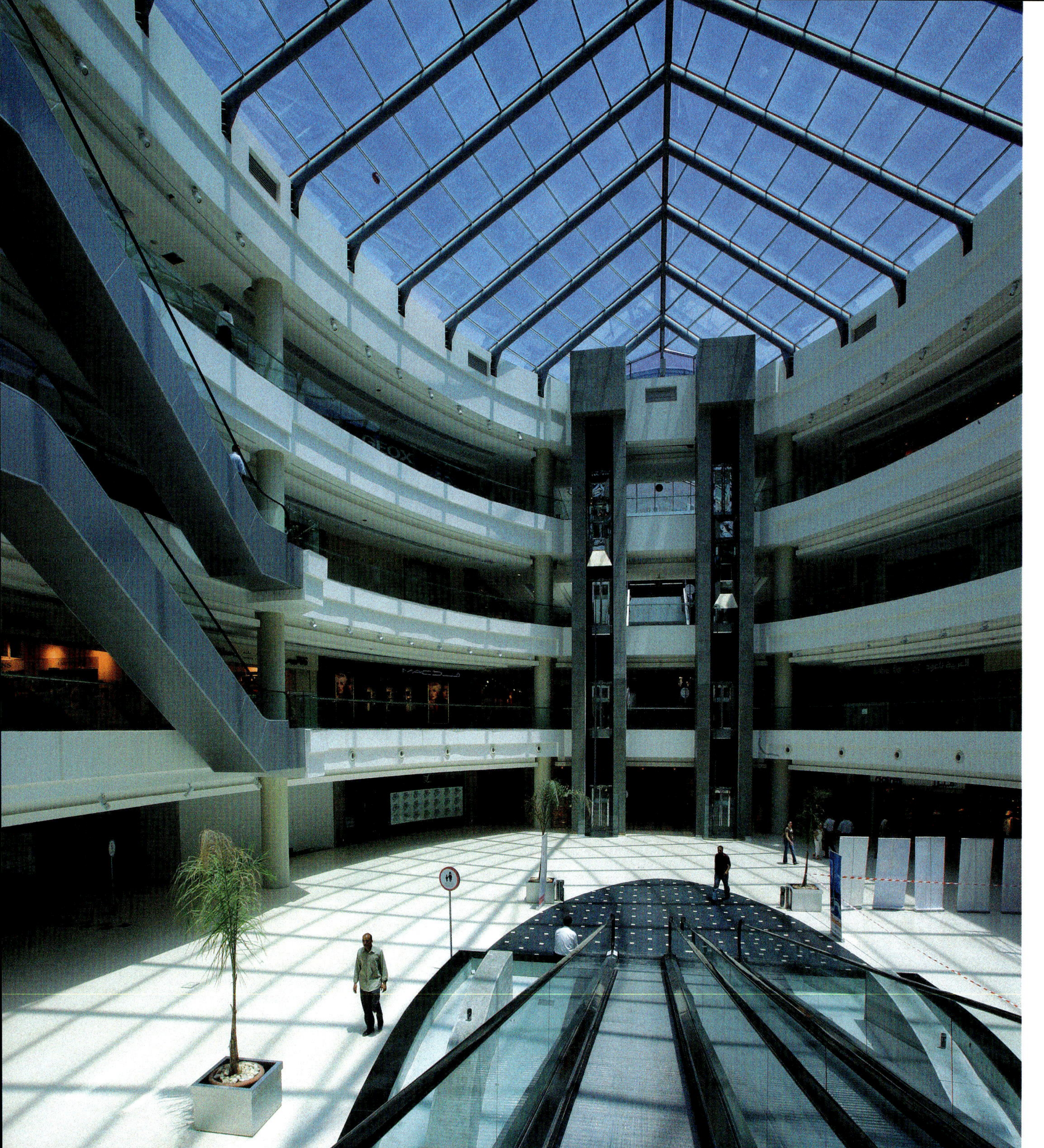

The colorful *souq* in downtown Amman is a striking contrast to the gleaming new mall. Both house a vast array of treasures, old and new.

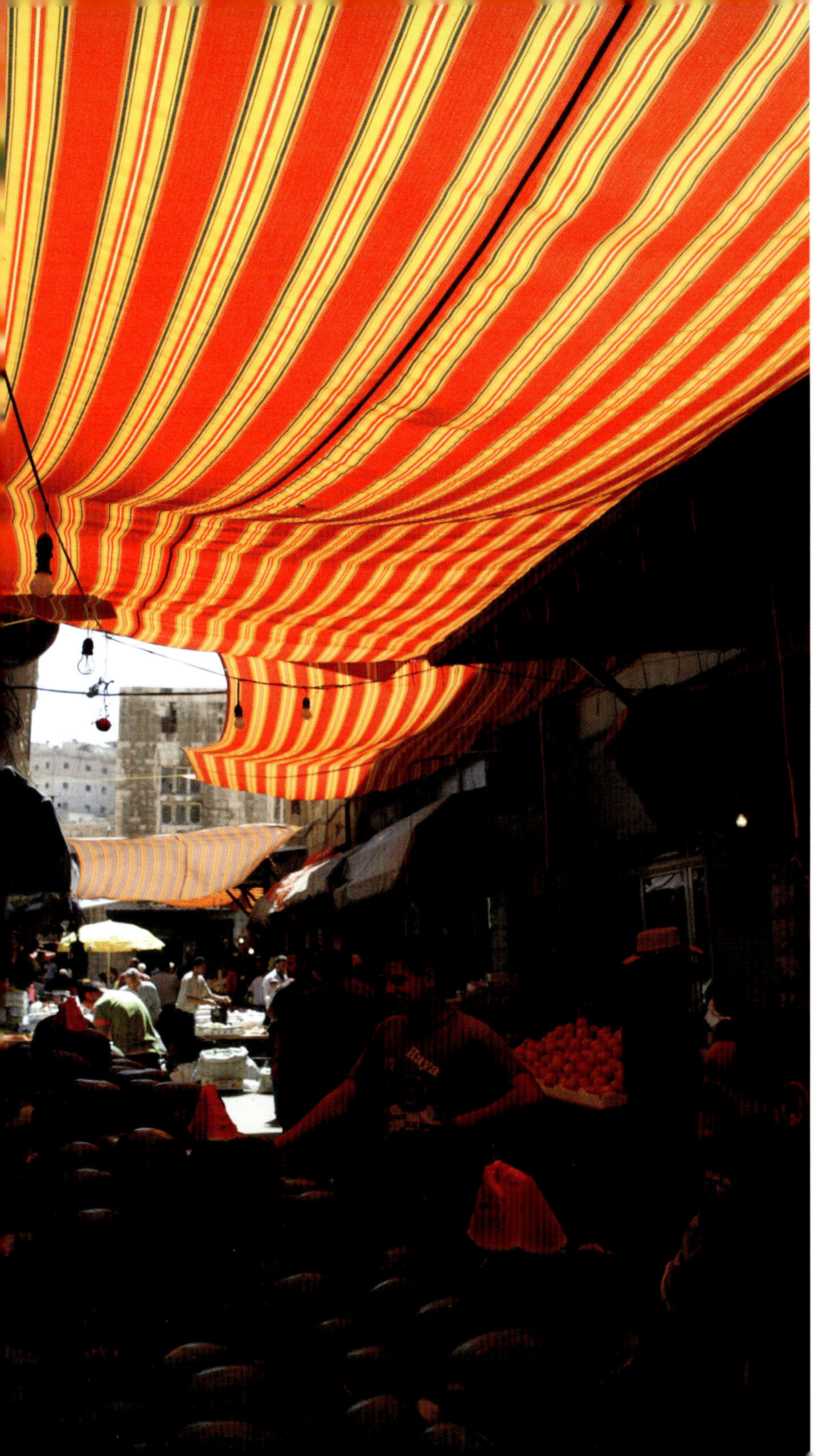

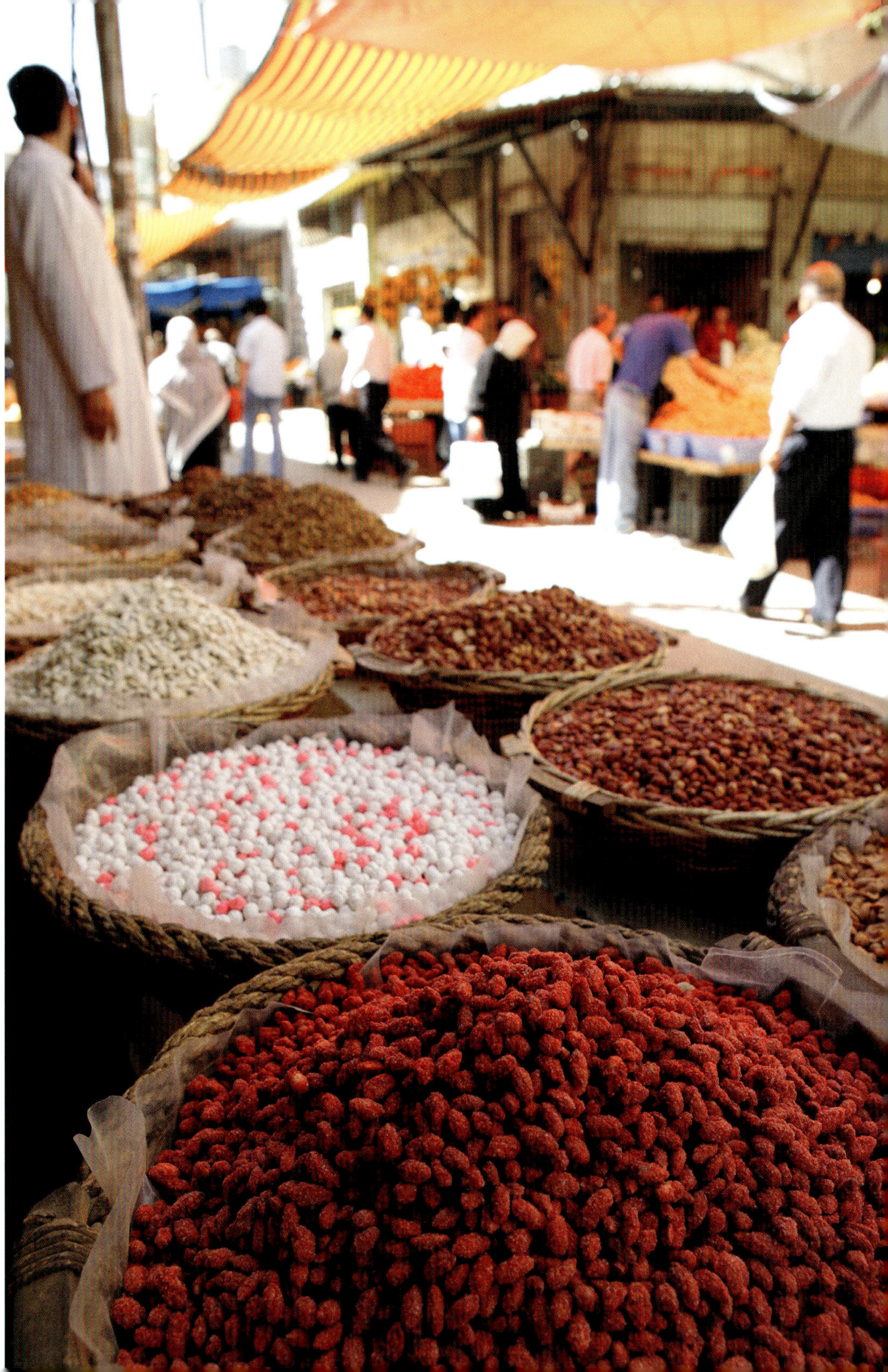

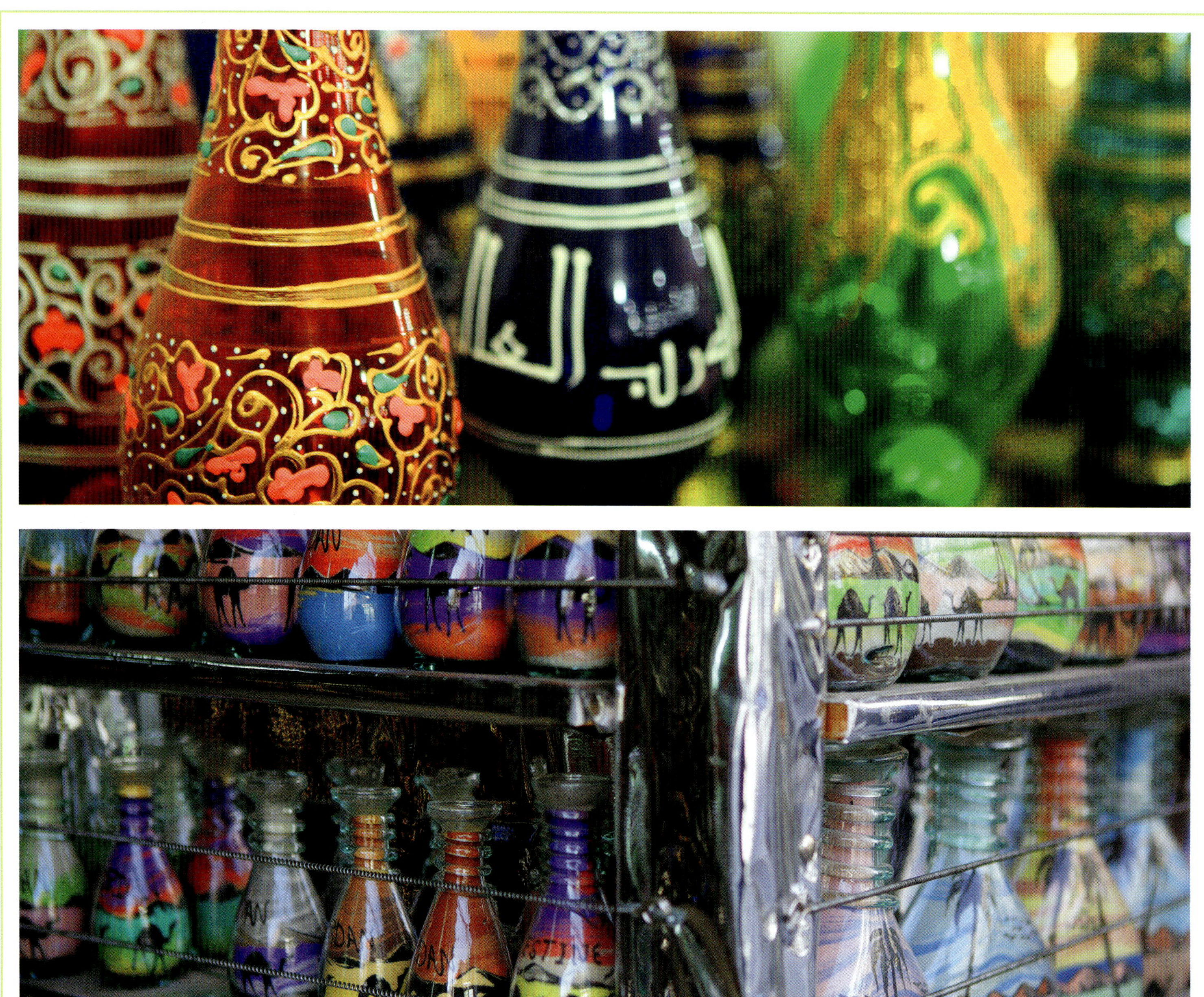

Rainbow colored glass handicrafts and sand bottles are some of the most popular souvenirs to be found in shops across Jordan.

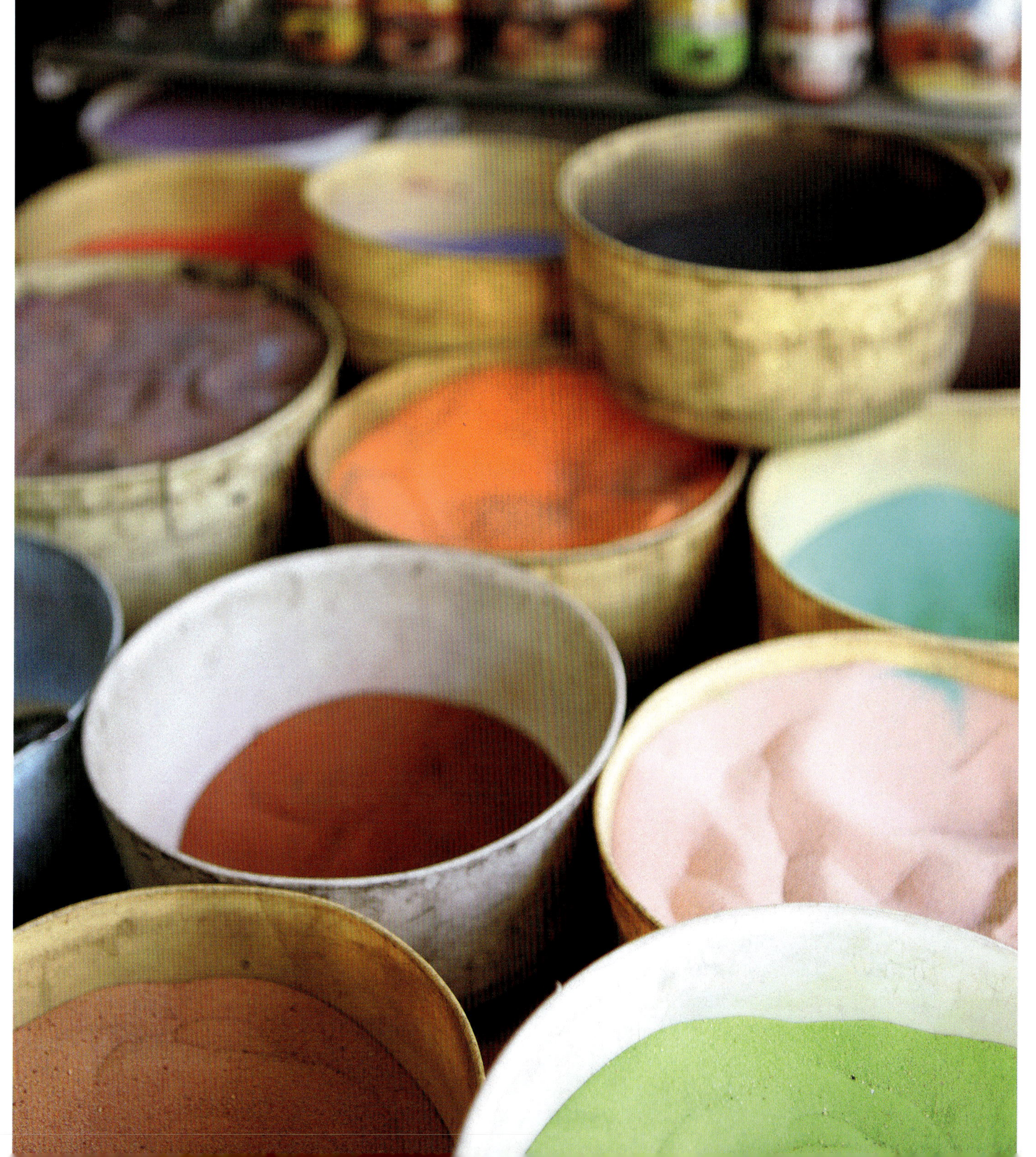

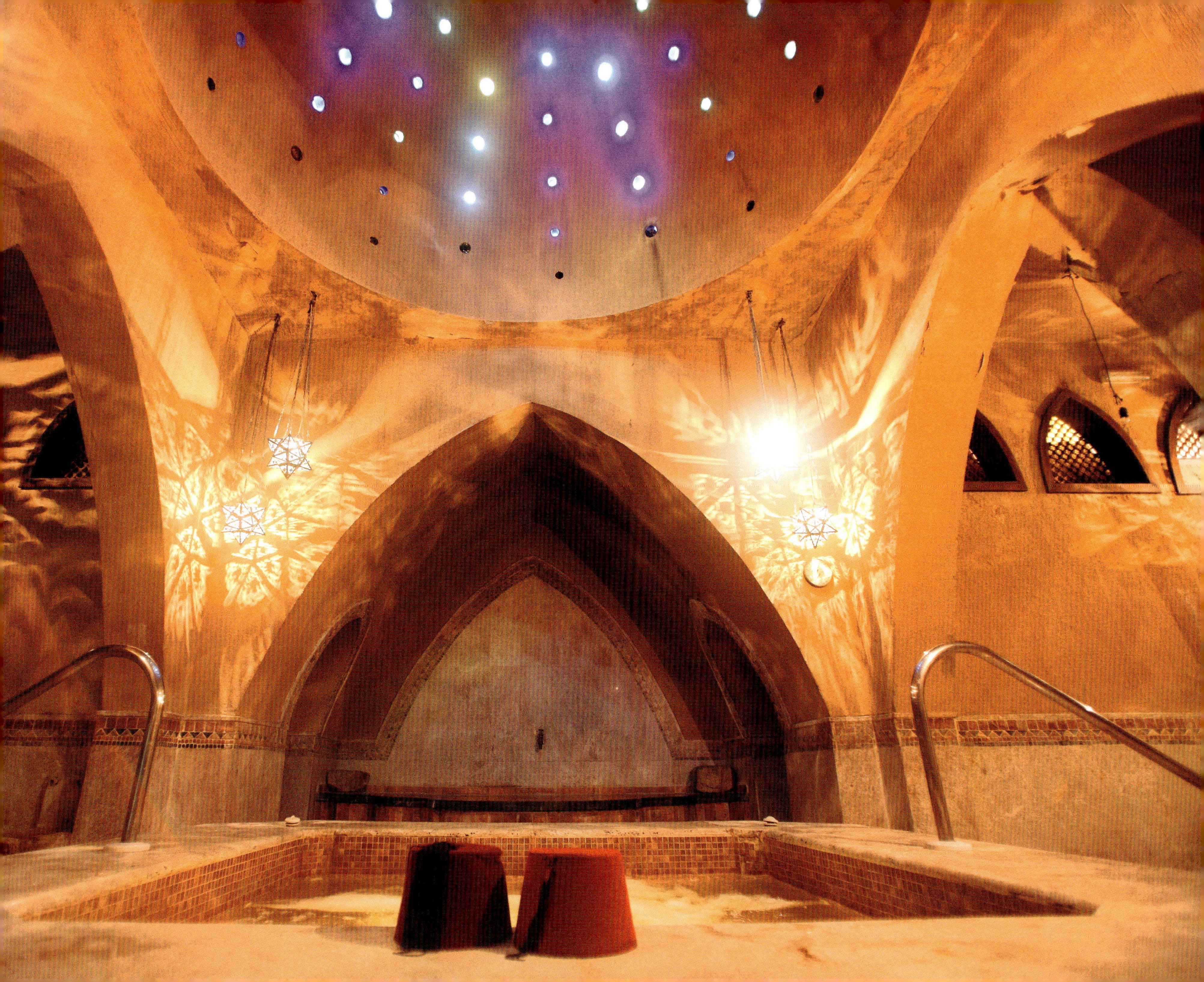

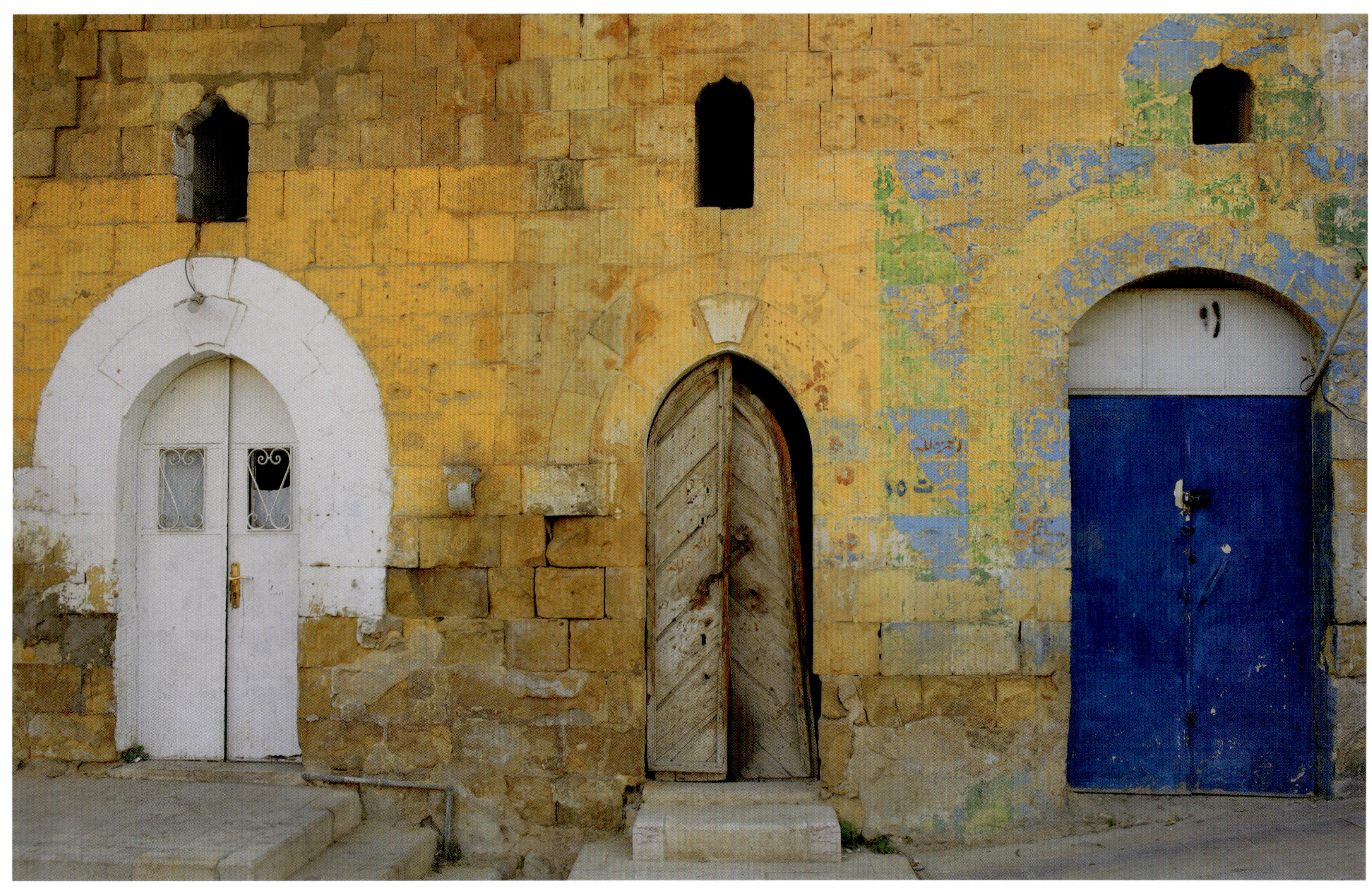

The only *Hammam* (Turkish Bath) in Amman – the El Pasha Turkish Bath – built in the Ottoman style, is a rich variety of ornamental designs that relieve the hustle of a day spent sightseeing.

Colorful doors in As-Salt, fashioned in the genre of the Ottoman Empire of the 1550s.

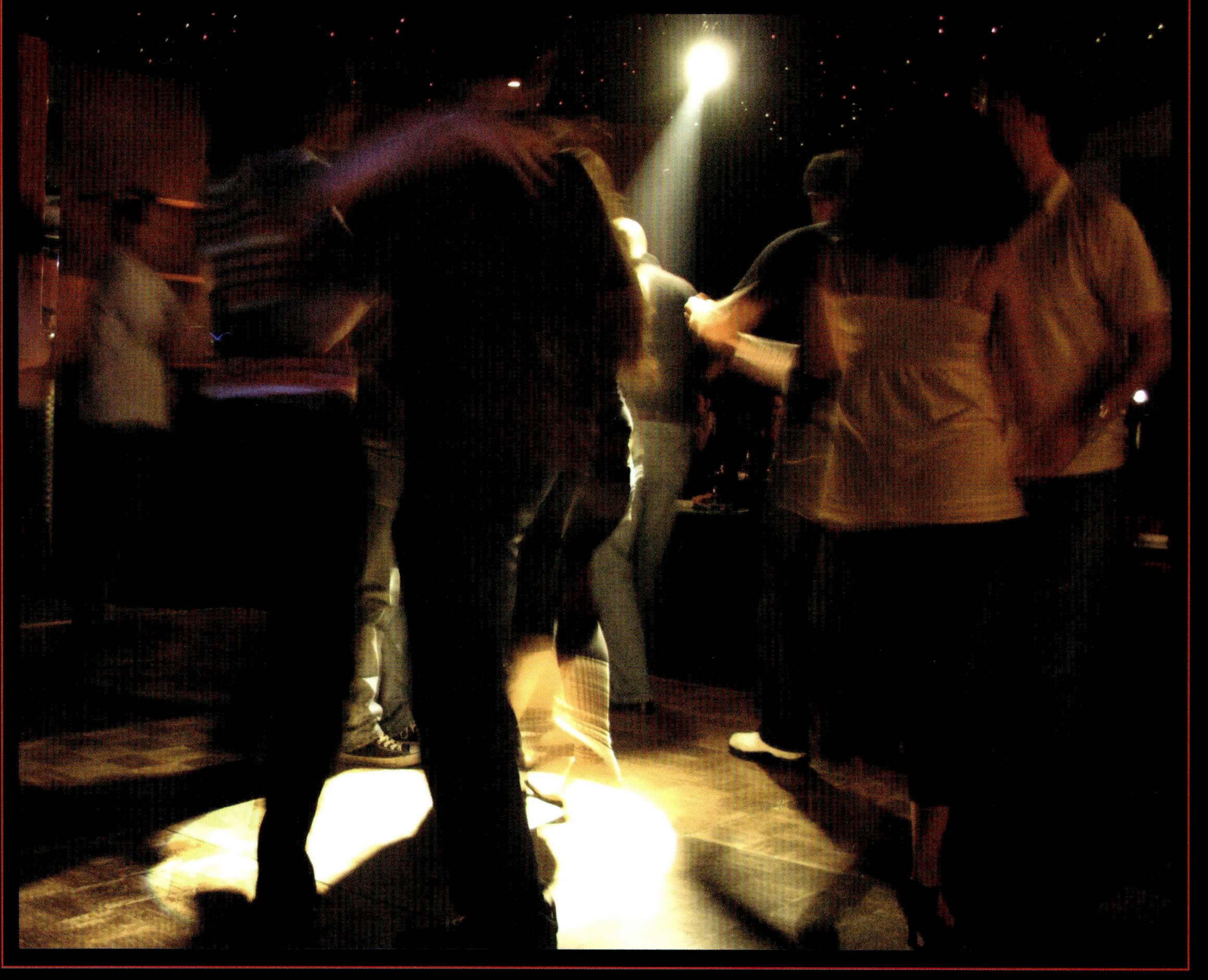

The modern, cosmopolitan capital city of Amman contains numerous outdoor cafés and restaurants where locals and tourists mingle on warm summer nights.

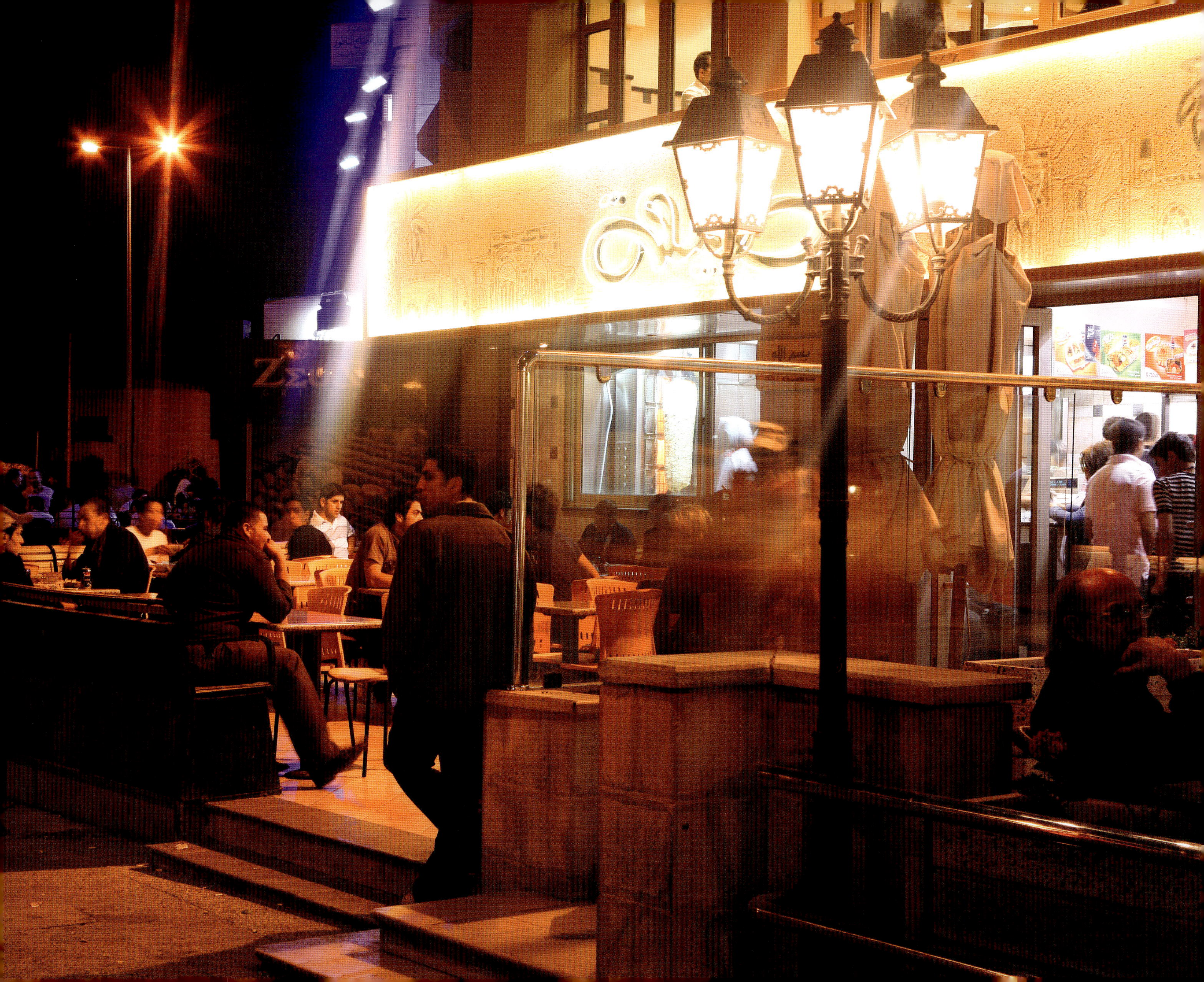

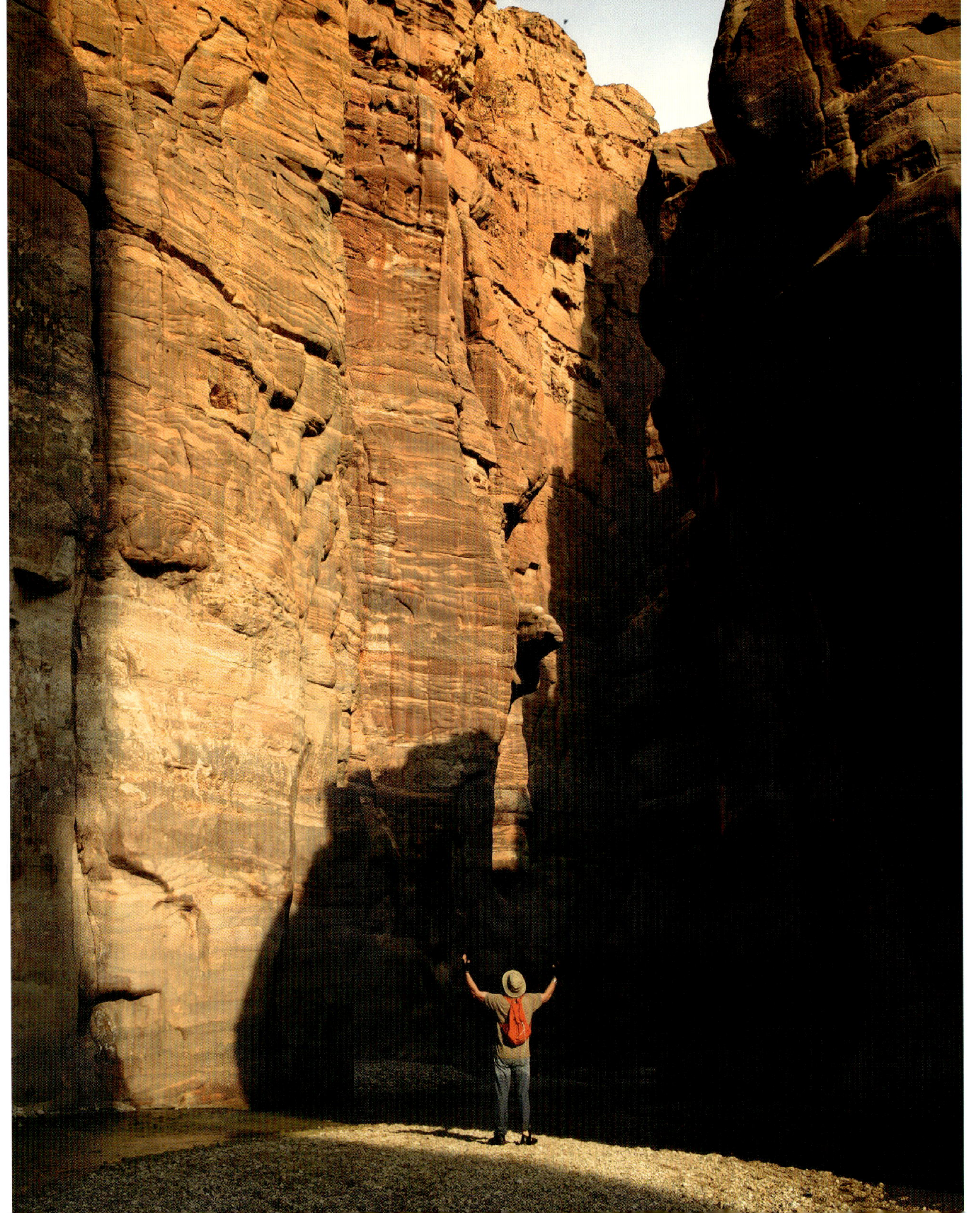

The soft, veined sandstone, adorning the walls of many tombs and chambers in Petra, is a masterpiece of rich red and orange earth tones.

Gorge walking routes, like this one in the Wadi Mujib, instill a sense of awe and appreciation for the work of art carved by Mother Nature.

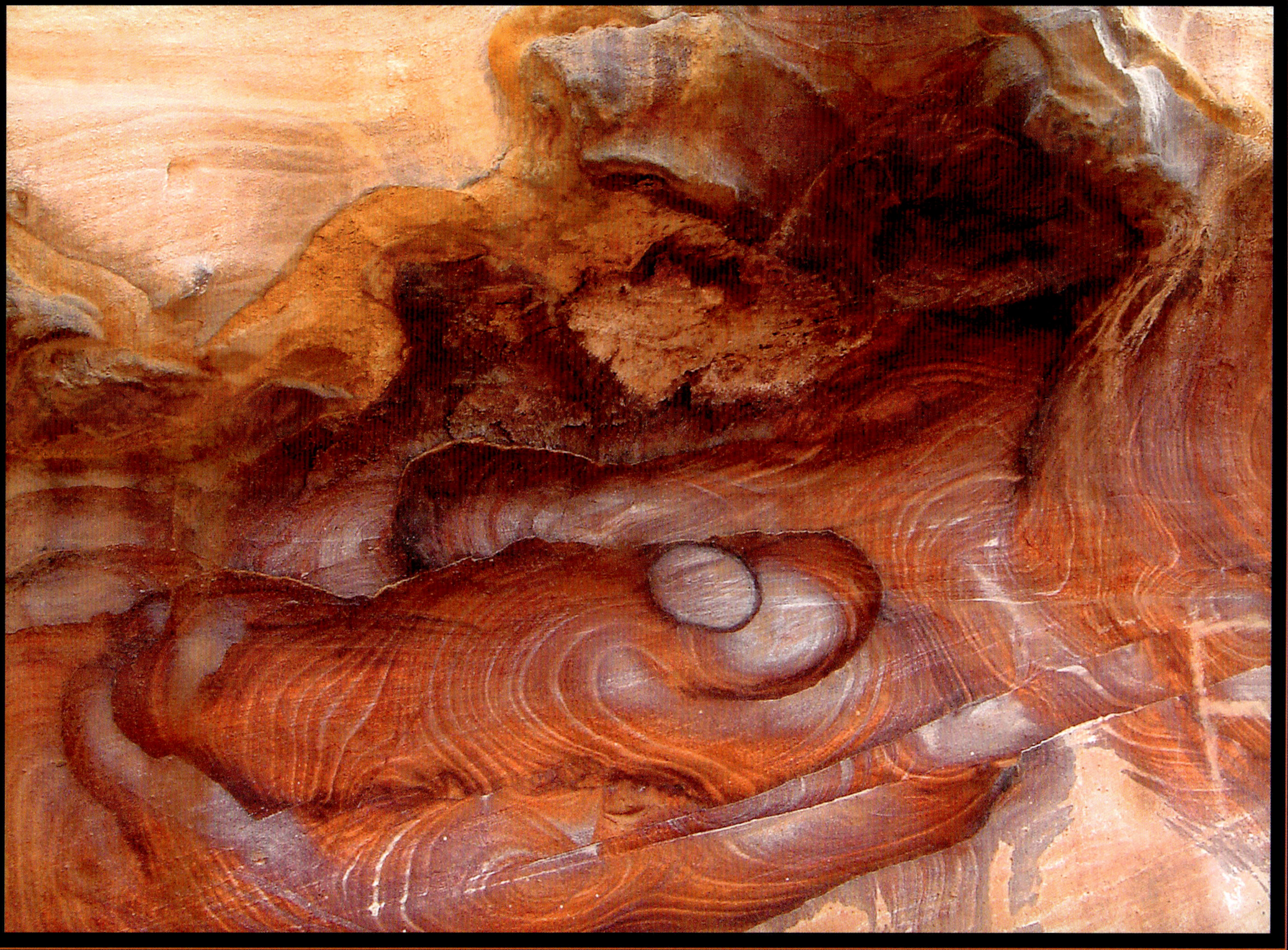

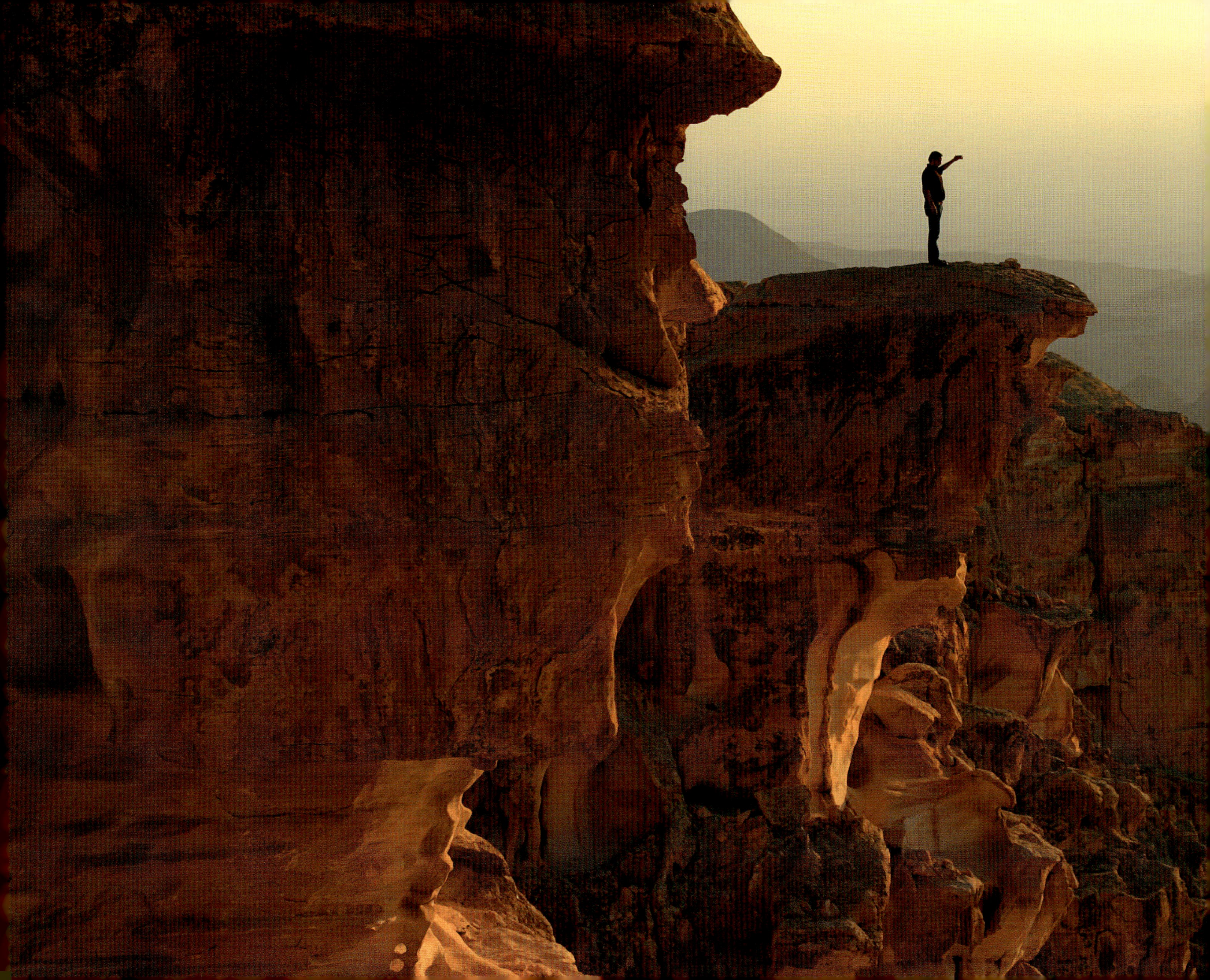

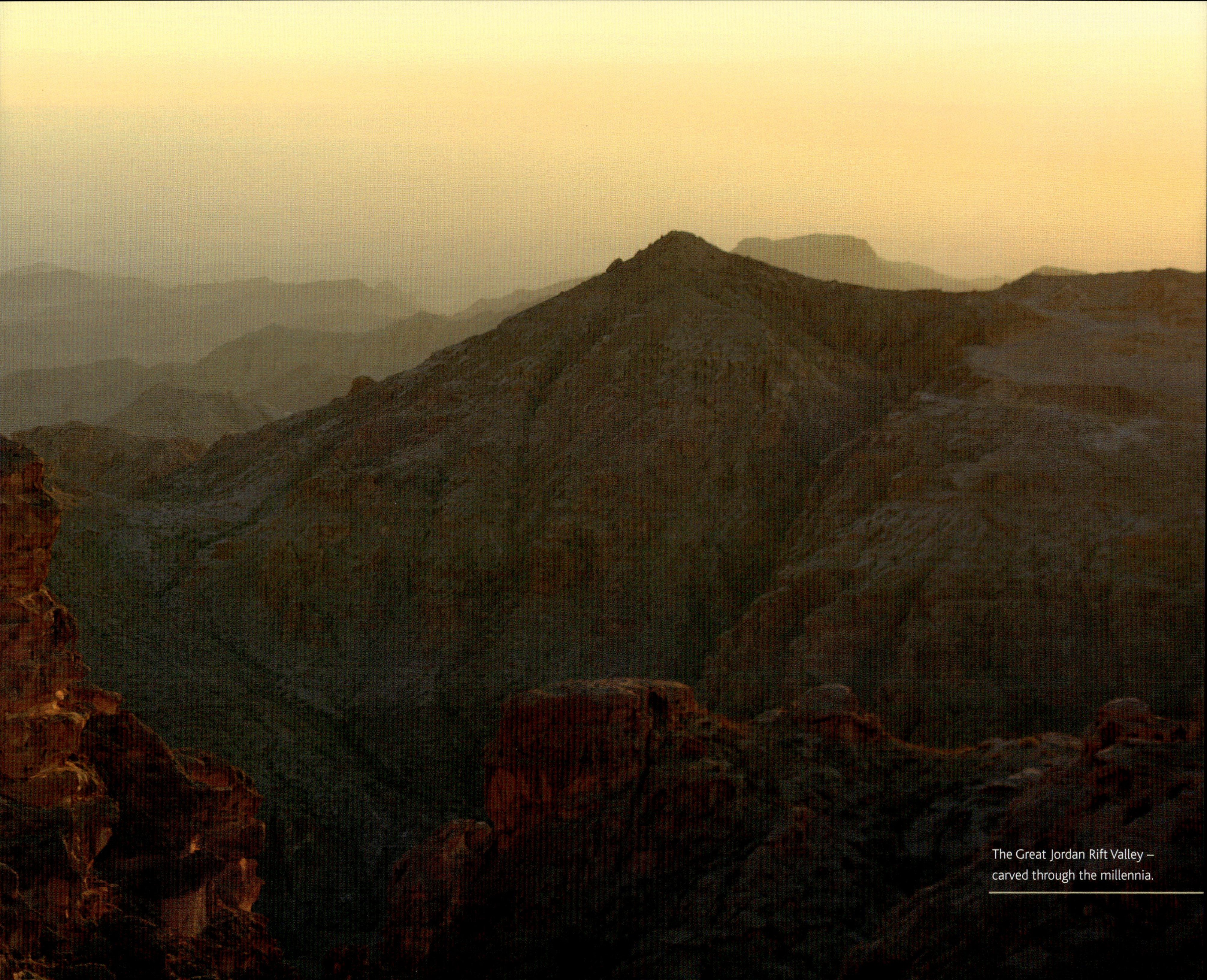

The Great Jordan Rift Valley – carved through the millennia.

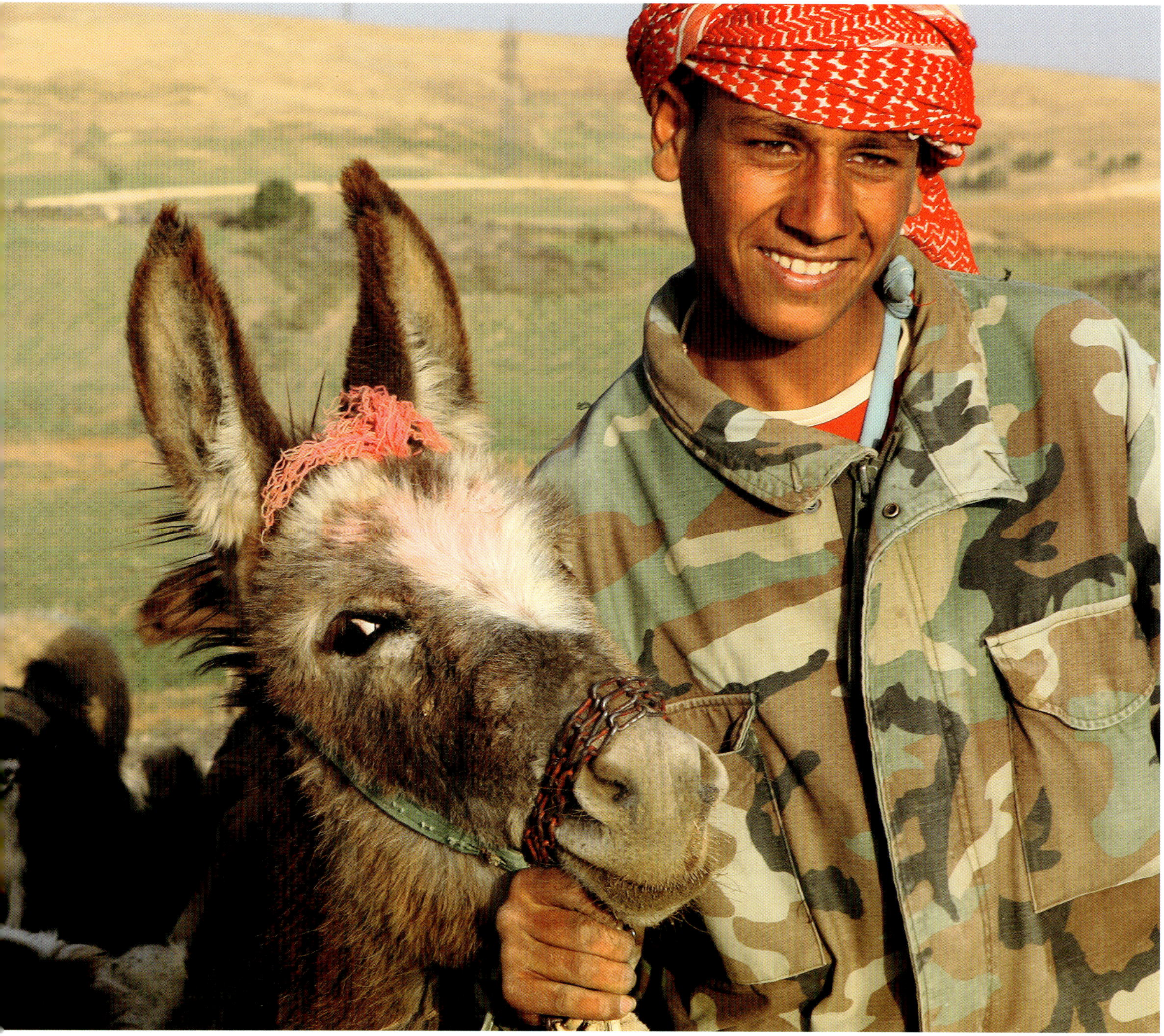

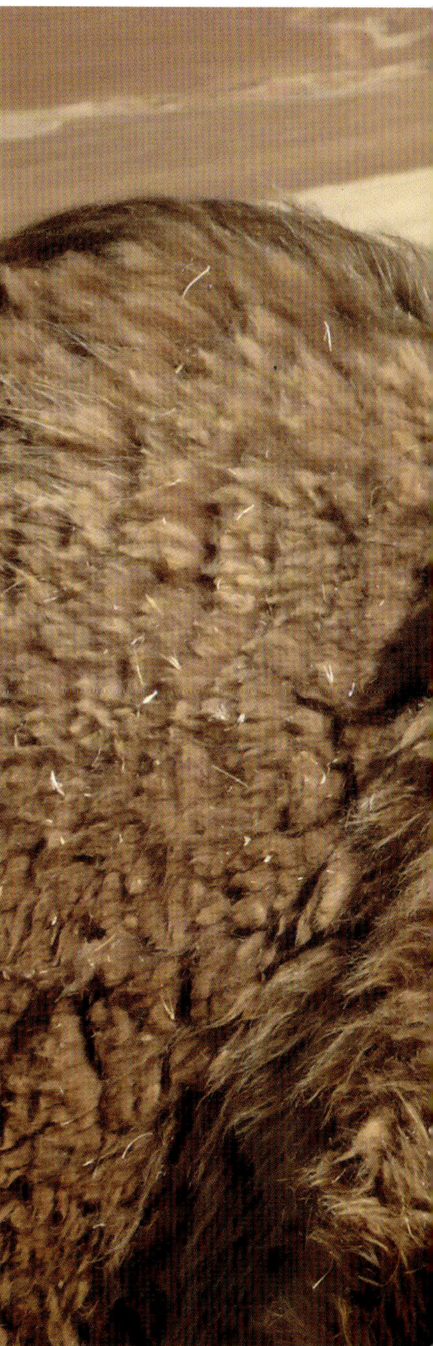

A young boy marches his flock of sheep to a desert market where Bedouins bargain on the price of each animal.

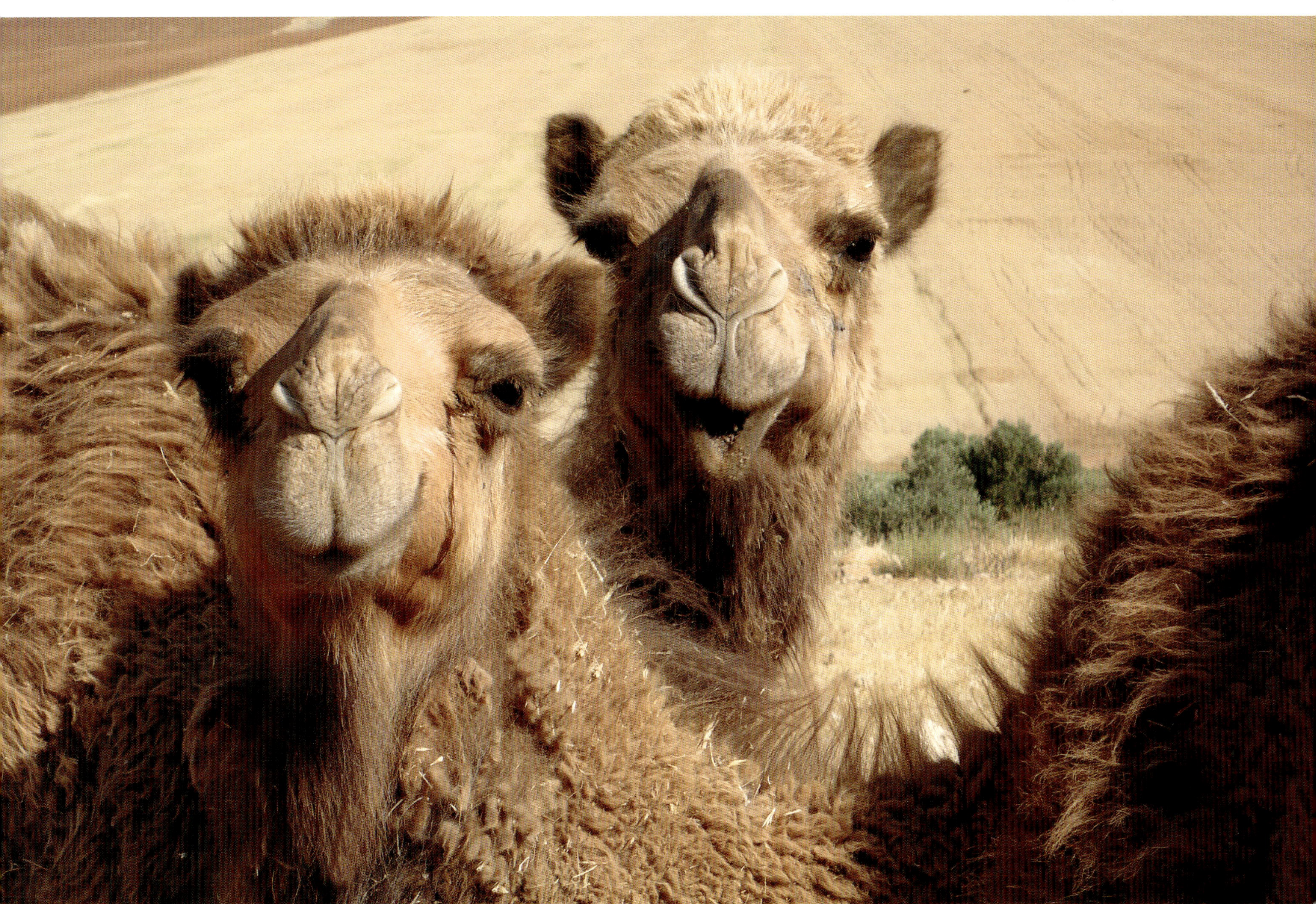

Curious camels appear to be smiling and posing for the camera.

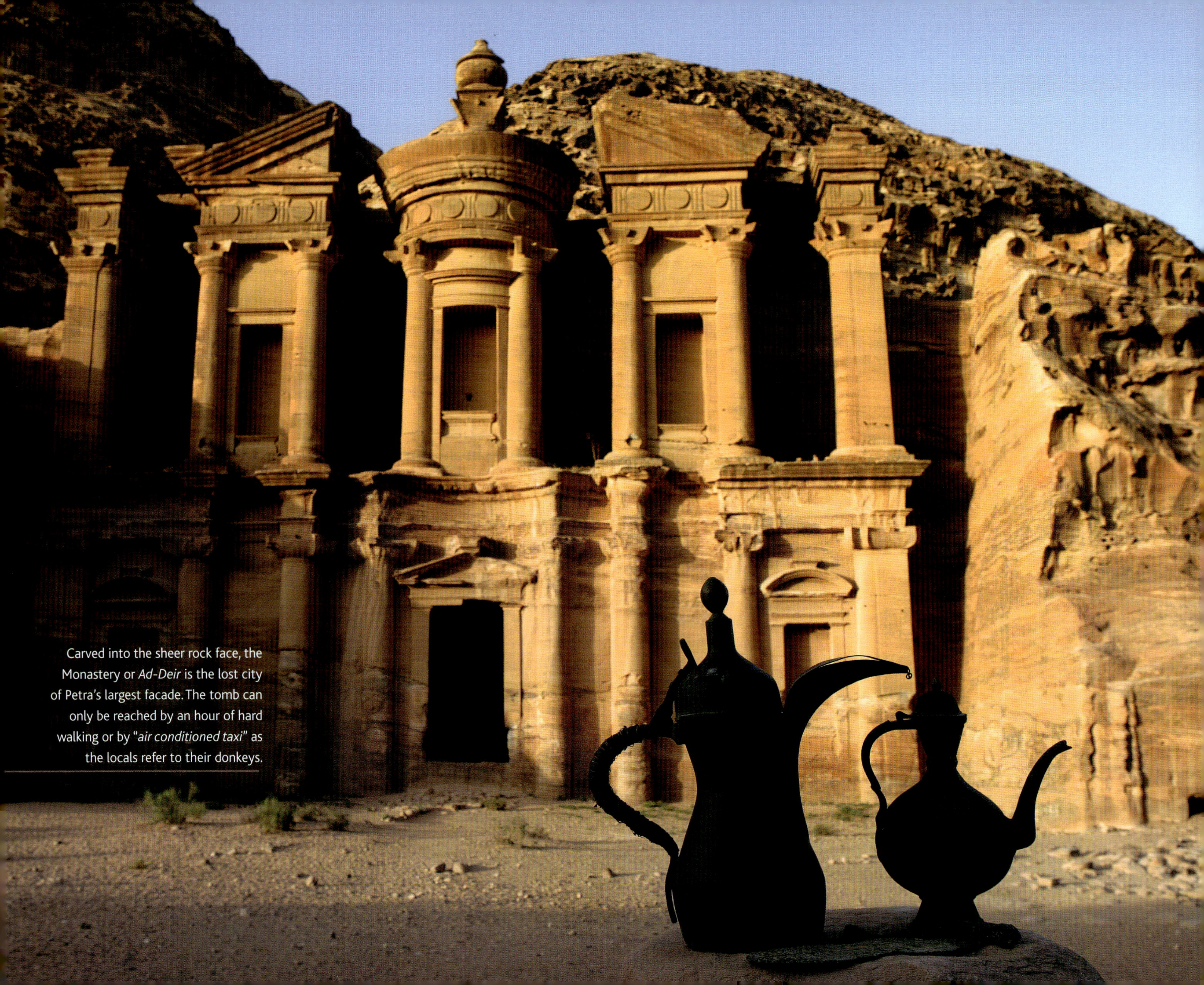

Carved into the sheer rock face, the Monastery or *Ad-Deir* is the lost city of Petra's largest facade. The tomb can only be reached by an hour of hard walking or by "*air conditioned taxi*" as the locals refer to their donkeys.

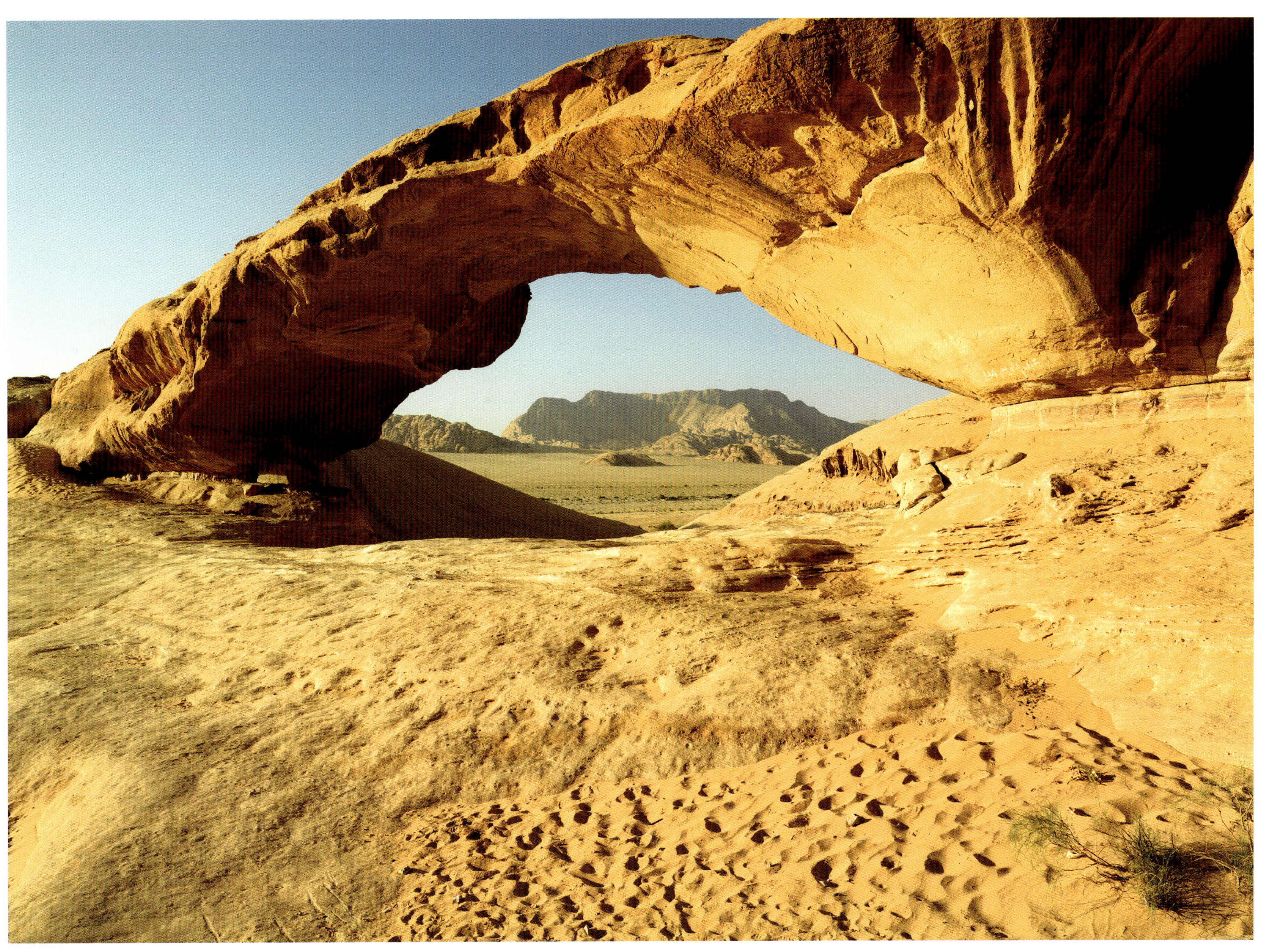

The north ridge of Jabal Burdah boasts one of the Wadi Rum's most impressive sites, the Natural Rock Bridge, a testimony to the chiseling effects of wind and water.

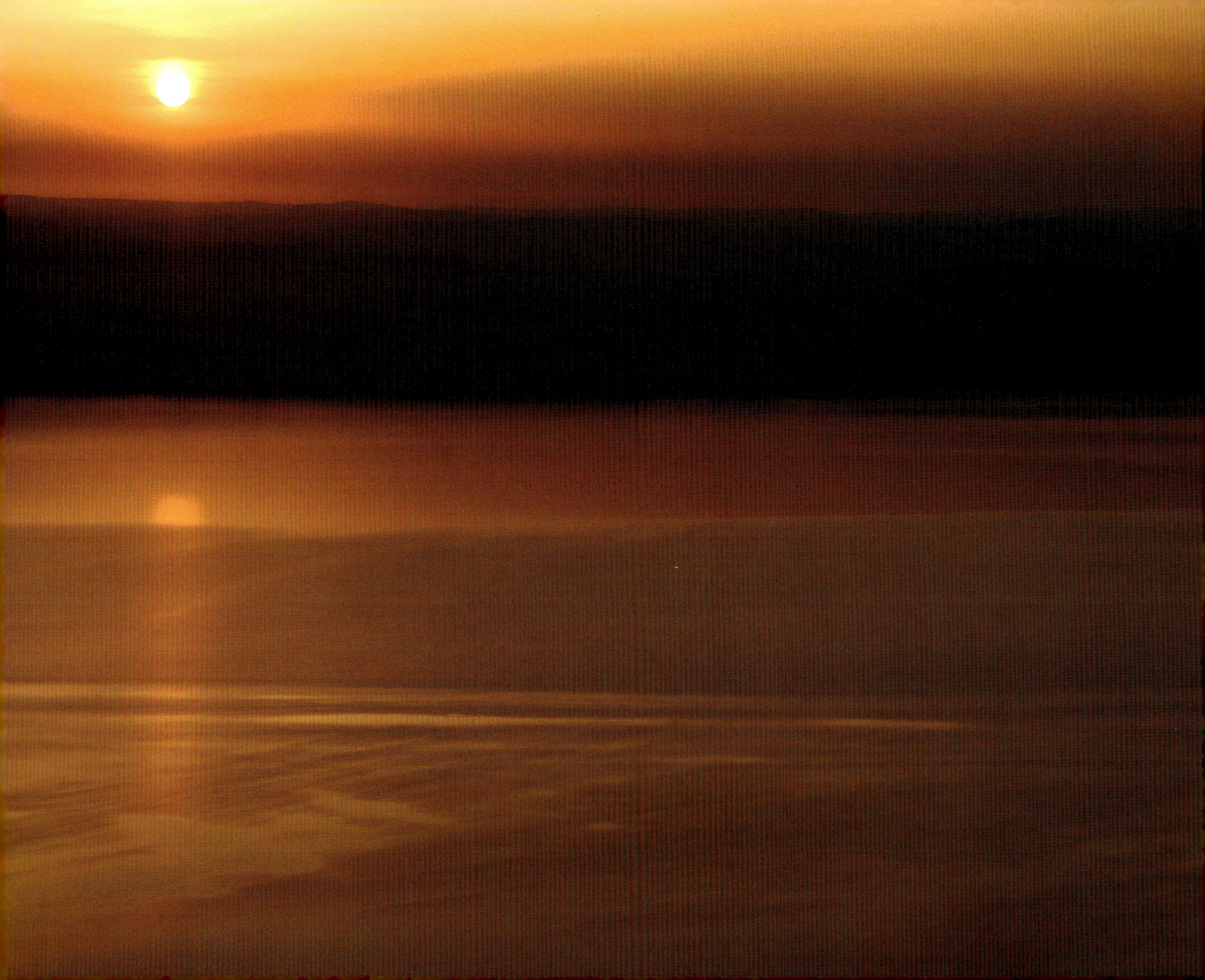

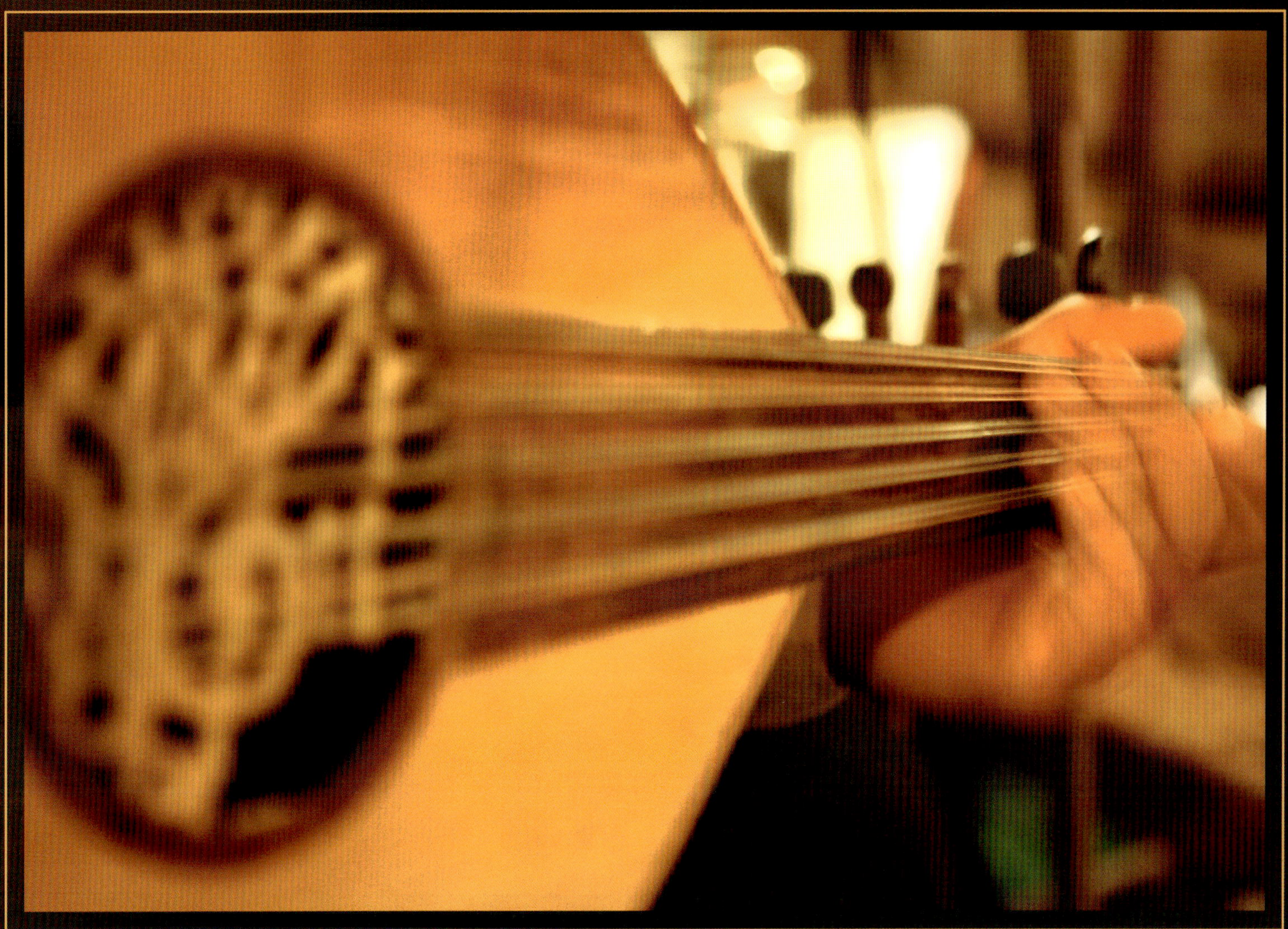

Kan Zaman, situated high atop a hillside just outside Amman, has become a popular tourist stop. Visitors can relax and enjoy a banquet of traditional Arabic foods while listening to a hypnotic melody played on the *oud*.

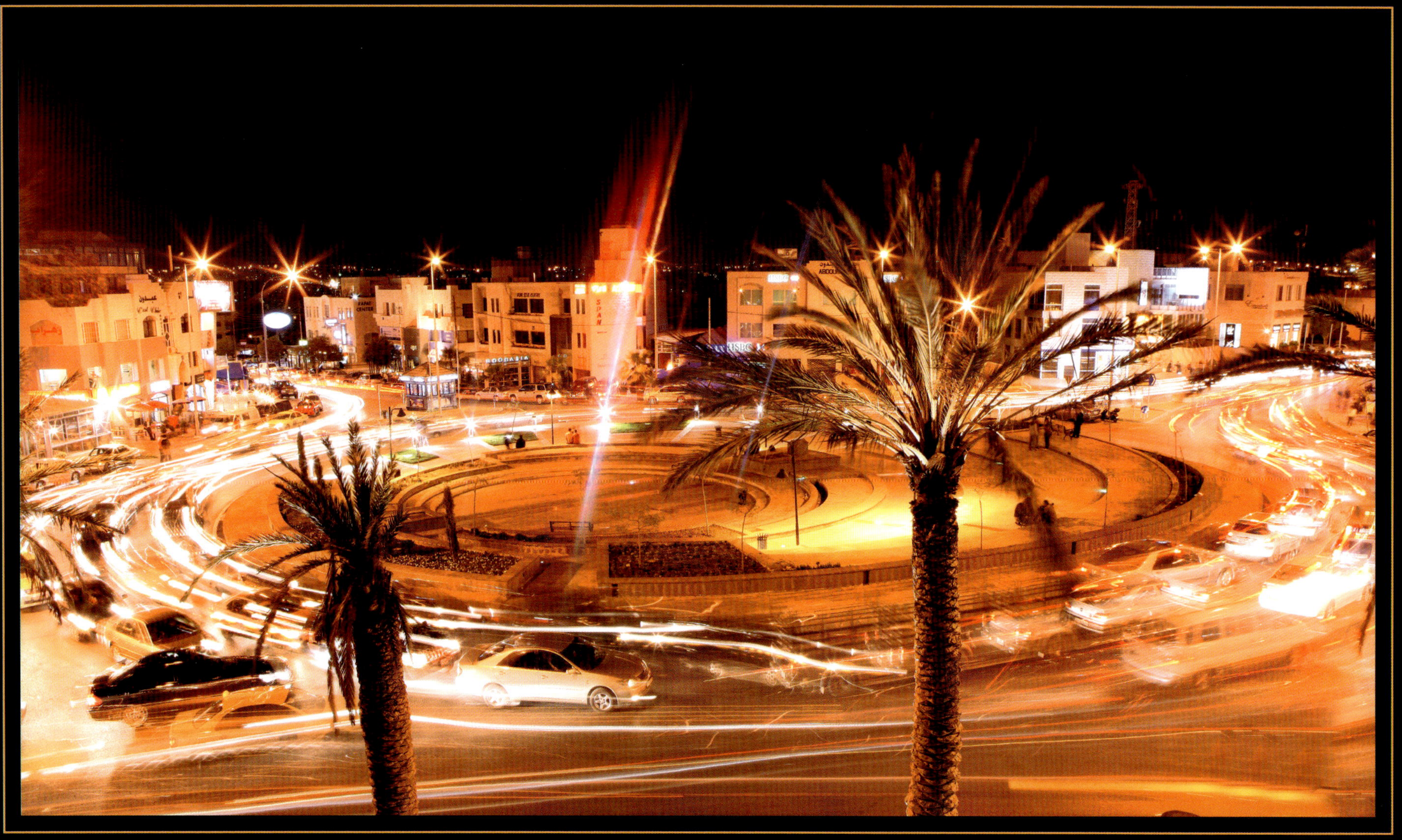

Abdoun Circle at night is a hub of cars, people and late night activity as Jordanians anticipate a night out on the town.